'I must have his eyes' – Herbert von Karaja
Peter Glossop on stage. He was searching for
new production of Verdi's *Otello* and had jusι ..ςςιι ςσπαuctıng *I Pagliacci*
with Peter Glossop, the first time he had encountered him. He probably
did not know that forty years earlier Peter Glossop had been born into a
humble family in the industrial city of Sheffield and had begun his life as a
bank clerk before joining the chorus of the Sadlers Wells Opera. From
these beginnings, he ultimately became acclaimed far and wide as one of
the world's most impressive dramatic baritones, a singer and actor of
commanding power and gripping subtlety. Even the fearsome audiences at
La Scala Opera House in Milan had taken him as their favourite Verdi
baritone, an unprecedented situation for an English singer, and something
the passionately determined Peter Glossop had never dreamed of when he
began his working life.

In this autobiography, Peter Glossop tells us the frank and unusual story
of an artist whose ascent to the heights was a long and arduous journey
through uncharted territories. It is a tale of a disarmingly straightforward
but deeply sensitive man who conquered the hallowed but intrigue-ridden
corridors of prestigious opera houses through the force and love of his art,
ultimately paying a price for his individuality and outspokenness.

Mr Glossop conjures up a vivid perspective on a legendary world that
has changed so vastly in his time. It includes his memories of the Sadlers
Wells Opera Company, the Royal Opera House Covent Garden, La Scala
Opera Milan and the New York Metropolitan Opera amongst other
international houses. There are personal recollections of singers such as
Placido Domingo, Luciano Pavarotti, Mirella Freni, Dame Gwyneth Jones
and Jon Vickers; conductors Otto Klemperer, Carlo Maria Giulini, Sir Georg
Solti, Herbert von Karajan and James Levine; and directors Franco Zeffirelli,
Luchino Visconti and Roman Polanski. There are discussions of some of
Mr Glossop's most celebrated roles, and an entire chapter is devoted to the
performance of Verdi, with analyses of parts such as Macbeth, Rigoletto
and Iago. There is also a chapter on Benjamin Britten, who selected Peter
Glossop for the title role in his recording of *Billy Budd* after telling him
'finally I have found my Billy Budd'.

Peter Glossop – the Story of a Yorkshire Baritone is a story of inspiration,
joy and suffering from a great and compelling artist with a profoundly
revealing overview of the music and people of his profession.

First published in 2004 by Guidon Publishing
23 West Street, Oxford OX2 0BQ

ISBN 0-9543617-3-3

Typeset by Antony Gray
Printed and bound in Great Britain by
Lightning Source

The front cover illustration shows Peter Glossop
as Rigoletto at the Parma Opera House, 1965,
by kind permission of the Teatro Regio, Parma

I dedicate this book to my mother,
Violet Elizabeth Glossop, without
whose belief in me and my voice
there would never have been
a story to write

Contents

	List of Illustrations	9
	Acknowledgment	11
	Preface by Lord Harewood	13
	Foreword by Sir Charles Mackerras	15
	Foreword by Sir Edward Downes	16
	Foreword by Bernard Keeffe	17
ONE	Prologue – Sheffield, Yorkshire	21
TWO	Sadlers Wells – The Journey Begins	34
THREE	Going to the Garden	68
FOUR	Covent Garden – Gateway to the World	89
FIVE	A Son of Italy	104
SIX	Some Thoughts on Verdi	117
SEVEN	Benjamin Britten – A Memoir	131
EIGHT	Around the World in Twenty Years	139
NINE	Goodbye to all That – Mostly	158
	Index of musical works	169
	Biographical index	171

List of Illustrations

A month before my twelfth birthday, June 1940   23

My first Principal rôle at Sadlers Wells –
    Morales in Carmen, 1953   41

With Joyce Blackham around the time of our engagement   45

Eugene Onegin, with Ava June as Tatyana,
    Sadlers Wells, 1962   57

The Sofia competition, 1961, with my Russian accompanist   63

Amonasro in Aida, Szeged, 1962   71

Rodrigo in Don Carlos, Royal Opera House,
    Covent Garden, 1968   84

Di Luna in Il trovatore, with Dame Gwyneth Jones as
    Leonore, Royal Opera House, 1964   99

Receiving an honorary degree from Sheffield University
    with, left to right, A. R. Clapham, W. H. Auden and
    Sir Kenneth Clark, 18 July 1970   105

Making up before going on the stage of La Scala Opera
    House as Rigoletto   112

Début at La Scala Opera House, Milan, 1965 – Rigoletto   113

A prized letter from Dietrich Fischer-Dieskau about my
    performance of Iago   125

Iago gloating over the unconscious Otello (Jon Vickers),
  Salzburg Festival, 1970   127

Recording Billy Budd   134

Wozzeck, *New York Metropolitan Opera, 1972*   143

Iago from the film Otello *directed by Herbert*
  von Karajan, with Jon Vickers as Otello   147

The French Governor of Sicily in I vespri Siciliani,
  Paris, 1974   150

Joyce Blackham in the role of Carmen   152

With Roman Polanski, Munich, 1976   153

With Michelle, Amber and Rosie   159

With Amber   161

Amber and Rosie   161

Acknowledgment

The author would like to thank Francesca Franchi, archivist of the Royal Opera House Covent Garden, Clare Colvin, archivist of the English National Opera, Robert Tuggle, archivist of the New York Metropolitan Opera, and Cosetta Vallerini, press director of the Parma Opera, for their invaluable assistance with information and photographs for this book.

Preface by Lord Harewood

'Discovery' is an ambivalent term when used in an operatic context. It can mean digging out an unknown opera that deserves to be staged; it can mean recognising the talents of a hitherto unknown performer; or it can simply mean finding a talent you yourself have not previously known but now find exciting. This last is what happened to my wife and me when we first heard Peter Glossop at Sadlers Wells, singing Eugene Onegin. Here was plainly a major talent – a beautiful baritone voice and an admirable stage performer. More than that: the rich, nutty sound of the voice itself gave immense pleasure; it was used with real skill and artistic purpose; it had attack and was consistent throughout a wide compass. What a discovery!

'Discovery' as a phenomenon inevitably wanes, but the pleasure you can get from your personal discovery persists over many years. We heard Peter in all sorts of roles, frequently in operas by Verdi – perhaps his major strength – and we enjoyed his contributions to each of these operas. We heard him in quite a number of theatres in several countries abroad, and the pleasure was duplicated when we heard him in *The Flying Dutchman* in Leeds and, less centrally for a Verdi baritone, as Mandryka in *Arabella* at the Coliseum with English National Opera. The latter was one of only two occasions when I had the pleasure of being involved in a management that was presenting him (the other was in my time at the Edinburgh Festival when he sang, soon after the memorable Onegin, Tarquinius in *The Rape of Lucretia* for the English Opera Group). In *Arabella* he filled with distinction a baritone role which is hard to cast, because of the range and personality required, and is also one of my absolute favourites in any opera by Richard Strauss. Here was the man of mystery Strauss and Hofmannsthal required, apparently coming from outer space (in this case, Yorkshire?); this was the man to sweep Arabella off her feet, as he had swept us off our seats more than twenty years before in London.

LORD HAREWOOD
July 2003

Foreword by Sir Charles Mackerras

What a pleasure it is to welcome Peter Glossop's auto-biography. I seem to have known him for so long that I cannot even remember the first opera we did together, but I know that over the years we did many Verdis, both in English and Italian, of which his Simon Boccanegra and his Italian Iago at Covent Garden and his English Iago on BBC TV stand out in the memory as the most beautifully voiced and stylishly sung Verdi from any British singer of that era.

His bluff, open manner made him in many ways an ideal Billy Budd, even if perhaps the basic innocence of the character eluded him. That nerve-racking BBC television recording with Ben Britten himself breathing down our necks and that final 'Starry Vere, God bless you' coming out loud and clear just as the clock reached eleven o'clock, is something none of us will ever forget.

Peter was a marvellous person to work with, very efficient, down to earth and always sensitive to the other singers with whom he was singing, although his habit of 'calling a spade a bloody shovel' caused some rifts with managements during his career. He had a great feeling for the Italian style and got nearer to the true Verdian 'Italianita' than any non-Italian baritone of his generation.

I am glad to read his interesting remarks on Verdi's *Macbeth*, an opera in which I heard him in both its versions, but which I never had the pleasure of performing with him.

This biography should be read by all young singers who would like to make a career on the operatic stage.

CHARLES MACKERRAS
July 2003

Foreword by Sir Edward Downes

From the late 1950s until the early 1980s we were fortunate at Covent Garden in having as company members – not just periodic guests – a handful of singers who in their particular vocal and dramatic categories had few equals anywhere in the world.

One notable member of the select group was Peter Glossop, and the publication of these memoirs will give great pleasure to his many admirers. They will remember the magnificent voice, the sometimes terrifyingly wild intensity of his dramatic character portrayals. They will also remember the great beauty of some of his quiet *legato* singing.

What they will not know, and may well be surprised to learn, is something that only those of us who have worked closely with him have long known and admired – that behind the brash, aggressive, barnstorming Yorkshireman was a fine natural musician and an artist of great sensitivity, humility, honesty, integrity – and even innocence! We should count ourselves fortunate to have known him.

EDWARD DOWNES
July 2003

Foreword by Bernard Keeffe

I was introduced to Peter rather indirectly when I was invited to be a member of the jury at the first International Opera Singers Competition in Sofia Bulgaria in 1961. The jury was eighteen strong; the bulk of them were from the Eastern Block, singers and conductors, but also included three from the West, the famous Italian soprano Toti dal Monte (then sixty-eight years old), the French baritone Camille Maurane, and myself. When I saw the list of entrants, I was intrigued to see the name of Peter Glossop. Of course I knew of him as a member of the Sadlers Wells opera company, but had never met him personally.

For the competition, the singers performed songs and arias in the preliminary rounds and the winners were then selected to take roles in a complete opera performance with the Sofia Opera. Peter made a very strong impression both on the jury and the audience, but after some complicated goings on with the jury, the competition was initially supposed to have been won by a Bulgarian baritone called Selimski. However, it was finally decided that Selimski and Glossop would be joint prize-winners. I heard later that the reason for this was that the local audience had made it clear that if Glossop did not win they would demonstrate. The Bulgarians on the jury could not contemplate a result for their first international competition that gave first prize to a singer from the West, so to try to get round the problem they insisted on joint winners.

Peter soon became internationally celebrated for his performances at the Royal Opera House Covent Garden. He benefited enormously from his studies in Italy – his naturally robust style was deepened and broadened to considerable effect, particularly in the demanding high baritone Verdi roles. So he was the obvious choice for a television programme, *Verdi and the Voice,* which I presented and conducted for the BBC. It was a very happy collaboration, with Peter in top form.

I find it extraordinary that neither Peter Glossop nor the late Charles Craig were given an official honour in recognition of their enormous contribution to opera – especially overseas, where their great talents did much to enhance the reputation of British opera singing. When I consider the worthy but minor local artists who have been honoured it seems that in Peter's time the powers that be were inclined to regard opera-singing, especially by such a robust character as Peter, as being less worthy than concert and oratorio. Had Peter sung Bach in the white English style, no doubt he would at least have been invited to Command the British Empire.

BERNARD KEEFFE
October 2003

PETER GLOSSOP
The Story of a Yorkshire Baritone

CHAPTER ONE

Prologue – Sheffield, Yorkshire

I was born to my parents, Violet Elizabeth and Cyril Glossop, in the Yorkshire city of Sheffield on 6 July 1928, in between the births of my brother Harry and my sister Doreen. We were situated in a pleasant suburb called Wadsley. The only draw-back of living there was that it was known solely for its hospital for insane people, which in those days was bluntly called the Wadsley Lunatic Asylum. At that time, the thought of a mental home caused embarrassment in my part of the world. When-ever I was asked where in Sheffield I came from and I replied Wadsley I was subjected to a chorus of laughter and my friends would look at the sky and pull funny faces. I quickly changed my district to Hillsborough.

Because Sheffield was a centre of iron and steel manu-facturing, it was not perceived as being a popular place, but it was in fact generally a respectable city with a good variety of shops and, on the whole, clean and neatly kept streets. The only real problem was smoke in areas that were near to the steelworks and the coal-producing sites. A man who lived opposite to me owned a furnace in Attercliffe, which was a particularly rough part of Sheffield and situated right in the middle of a heavily industrial area. His business made him prosperous, like many people with similar businesses in Sheffield, but he could not wait to leave work at the end of the day as it was so unpleasant there. Of course, a large part of the workforce in Sheffield spent eight hours a day, five days a week, in these conditions, so in truth the city was a mixture of good and bad. However, although times were hard, as a whole Sheffield was far more prosperous than it was after the war. After 1945, the Americans started building new factories in Japan producing cheaper cutlery and Sheffield's major industry was cut off in its prime just when it needed to recover from all the bombing it had suffered during the war.

Our happy family suffered a great tragedy when my father died at just thirty-three years old from tuberculosis. I was five and hardly knew that it had happened so it did not have a great impact on me at the time. But a year or two later I began to understand that there was no longer a bread-winner in the house. At the time of his death my father was the manager of the silver department of John Turton and Co. Ltd, one of Sheffield's leading cutlery manufacturers. His demise came as a terrible double blow because as well as being a devoted husband and father he had been a fine provider for the family whereas my mother, who was twenty-eight, had never had a job in her life and now suddenly had to bring up three children entirely on her own.

The change was traumatic as the family had been well placed. My grandmother's nephew became the Lord Mayor of Sheffield and was also the managing director of John Turton and Sons. Sheffield was a world cutlery centre at the time, so with this and my father's position as director of the silver department we had been fortunate to have good connections. For example, on my parents' wedding day the firm produced a special gift: a 120-piece mahogany case, handmade with electroplate nickel silver, ivory handles and the letter G, for Glossop, engraved on every handle. There were just two cases

*A month before my
twelfth birthday,
June 1940*

made like this – the other one was sent as a present to the
Queen. So when my father died, overnight we went from good
luck to bad luck and one of the most awful experiences my
mother recalled from this time was when she went to see my
father's uncle for advice. She also hoped he might help her find
a job. His answer was 'Really things are very difficult these
days.' (it was 1933) 'The only advice I can give you is to marry
again.' This to a grieving widow! She never forgave him.

Bessie, my mother, now decided that the only option was
to learn to type and become a receptionist. Meanwhile, my

grandmother, grandfather and uncle were obliged to come into our home to help out and so suddenly there were seven of us in a small semi-detached house. Even when my grandfather died, it was difficult with the six of us. But there was no alternative as my father left a large mortgage on the house that still had to be paid. Times were hard for my mother and it was very tough for all of us until my sister and I started to work much later on.

Looking back, though, I think I had a happy and easy-going childhood. I was educated at High Storrs Grammar School, but I wasn't an intellectual type and I had an out of doors life, playing with a ball, sliding on a sledge down hills in a field and that sort of thing. I was not much interested in school studies, but after just one year at school something was introduced that really did engross me. It was called music! It was dropped soon after because of the outbreak of war in 1939, which meant that there had to be cuts and music was one of them. But in that year I had the opportunity to do some singing, and in fact I performed part of Schubert's great song *Der Erlkönig*. My mother had been teaching me singing and I loved this strange and disturbing song about a father riding through a forest at night with his young child in his arms, desperate to protect him from the clutches of the evil Erlking spirit. Actually, what happened was that the parts of the child and the Erlking were split up between two boys in our class, and I remember I was the Erlking.

Not long after that my music education at school stopped abruptly, but a couple of years later something else came up at school that was just as special to me: drama. There was a lot of Shakespeare and as I was the best reader in the form of thirty-three pupils, I was given the best parts to read. At thirteen years old I was so at home with *Macbeth* that many years later when I came to perform Verdi's *Macbeth* I already knew everything about the character, unlike most singers who have to start at the very beginning. These were the seeds of my future passion for opera, which came out of my love of drama more than singing, really. I have always said that in opera, acting is equally as important as singing.

Then my poor brother died aged just sixteen years old. Just as it had been with my father, it was tuberculosis that killed him. They said in those days that tuberculosis was hereditary and because of this my future wife, Joyce, never obtained her father's permission to marry me. We had to wait until she was twenty-one years old and free to decide for herself before we could have our wedding. Twenty years later I was with Joyce on a flight to Bologna to sing Verdi's *Rigoletto* and I had such a heavy cold that I couldn't breathe properly. The captain was so concerned that when we landed at Bologna airport there was an ambulance waiting for us on the tarmac and they whisked Joyce and me off to the hospital. After taking some X-rays they discovered some scars on my lungs. They were the remnants of when I had been a victim of tuberculosis in my late teens and fortunately they had healed naturally. I was immediately given treatment and although I had to cancel the first night of *Rigoletto* I was well enough to sing the remaining performances. And I was not the only one of my father's offspring who had contracted tuberculosis. Not long after the end of the Second World War, my sister had to go into a sanatorium for six months with the same illness. So, my wife's father was not far out.

Eventually, in 1941, my mother obtained a job as secretary to the manager of the Lyceum Theatre in Sheffield. I was thirteen when this happened and a vitally important experience was to come out of it for me. My mother decided to smuggle me up to 'the gods', the amphitheatre at the top of the

Lyceum, to see all the visiting companies that came to Sheffield each year. Amongst them were the D'Oyly Carte and Carl Rosa Companies. The D'Oyly Carte brought the Gilbert and Sullivan operettas and the Carl Rosa brought grand opera. The Carl Rosa was a remarkable touring company that gave large numbers of people in many parts of England their first taste of opera, and I was one of them. I went to see *Rigoletto* and I was thrilled. From that moment I was completely taken over by opera. I went to every performance the Carl Rosa Company was giving in Sheffield that week and I decided I must be an opera singer. Years later I told the Maltese baritone Joseph Satariano, who was singing Tonio in the Company's performances of Leoncavallo's *I Pagliacci* in Sheffield, that it was his performance of the Prologue that had put me on the road to being an opera singer. He was a true acting singer with a thrilling theatrical presence. He was also the Rigoletto that week, so to this day he remains a unique part of my life – not least because Tonio and Rigoletto were to be two of my favourite and most successful roles.

There was also someone else who will always stand out as a major influence in my life and that was my mother. She unfailingly encouraged me to sing. 'Your father was a baritone,' she would say, 'and you will be a baritone, but when you get to fourteen and your voice breaks you must stop singing and let your voice rest for two years.' As well as always believing in my future as a singer, she gave me the most invaluable advice for my development. Many times in my life she was to support me in this way and I am eternally grateful and indebted to her.

I followed my mother's advice and stopped singing for two years when my voice began to break. When I was sixteen, I left school and found a job at Mappin and Webb, the cutlery manufacturers. I wanted to be an international travelling sales-man for them and was told that I had to be an office boy first of all, but after six months I realised that I had been told a lie. All they wanted was an office boy, so I left and joined the National Provincial Bank. Meanwhile, now that my voice had fully broken, a friend of mine suggested I see his father, who was the best-known baritone in Sheffield.

This is how I started to take regular singing lessons, with Leonard Mosley. He was a fine teacher and I started to make fast progress but unfortunately it could not last long because after eighteen months I had to join the army – national conscription in England still had another fifteen years or so to run before it was abolished. It was maddening that I could not continue with my singing lessons but, although some people tell horror stories about the army, I have to say that I found the experience useful and even enjoyable.

I was also very lucky because I was stationed in Dusseldorf and the Opera House and the large club that was converted into the officer's club were the only two major buildings standing after all the war damage – this was in 1946. Every week I went to the opera and I remember once going to see Verdi's *Don Carlos*, which was performed in German over there at that time. There was a superb bass called Helmut Fehn singing King Philip the Second and he made a tremendous impression on me. Twenty years later when I made my debut at the Dusseldorf Opera House singing Iago in Verdi's *Otello*, the day before the performance a friend and I were backstage in the Opera House and I asked him if he could maybe find out whether there was a remote chance that this bass might be around somewhere. My friend introduced me to a group of people in the artists' café: 'This is Mr Glossop, he is singing Iago here tomorrow night. He is wondering if anyone might know of a bass called Helmut Fehn.' Immediately an elderly man said 'Do you see that white-haired old man in the corner?

That is Helmut Fehn.' I went straight up to him and told him how much I had admired his King Philip twenty years ago. He was very moved – as I was.

When I came out of the army in 1948, I started work at the bank again – if you had to leave employment to do National Service, the employer was required by law to take you back after your two years in the army. I also started to play the cornet in a jazz band. During my time in the army I had discovered New Orleans jazz and as I had already learned how to play the bugle I was quite easily able to teach myself how to play some rudimentary jazz. A group of friends and I formed ourselves into The Tin Roof Jazzmen and for the next four years we played in dances and jazz clubs in whatever spare time we could find outside our day jobs. In my case there was precious little of that because I had quickly arranged to start singing lessons again with Mr Mosley.

This was the most important priority of all for me, but after six months I had become very depressed. Mr Mosley felt my voice had deteriorated beyond rescue during my time in the army and it was pointless my thinking of becoming a professional singer. He suggested I should continue to work in the bank and be satisfied with being an amateur singer. On my return home I told my mother that if that were the case I would give up singing entirely. If I could not be a professional I would rather not sing at all. She immediately telephoned Mr Mosley and read him the riot act. She also told him that she was a singer herself and was convinced that she could hear something special in my voice. As a result, lessons with Mr Mosley recommenced. My mother had fought for me and had she not done so on that occasion I do not think I would ever have become a professional singer.

I continued with Mr Mosley for another six months before

he retired and then I decided I wanted to study with Eva Rich, who was the best-known singing teacher in the North of England. She was also the Music Director of the Teacher's Operatic Society of Sheffield, which annually booked the Lyceum Theatre for a week of operettas and musicals. She accepted me as a pupil and so for the next three years I slaved away at my studies and earned my living at the bank during the day. After about a year, as Eva Rich realised I was most of all interested in opera, she sent me to audition for a Madam Scaife, who was the Music Director of the Sheffield Singers Operatic Society. They performed an opera each year in the Montgomery Hall, a convenient small theatre in the centre of Sheffield. I sang an audition for the chorus to about five people, and when I finished they all huddled together to talk in a corner of the room. Eventually Madam Scaife came over to me and asked if I would sing a principal role. I was staggered as I had only come to audition for a place in the chorus but I immediately said 'yes!'

The forthcoming production was Offenbach's *The Tales of Hoffman*. In this opera all four baritone roles are usually taken by the same singer, but in amateur companies they are usually cut to just three and taken by different singers to give more people an opportunity. However Madam Scaife offered me two character roles, Coppelius and Doctor Miracle. And so it was that I sang my first opera performances on stage at the age of twenty-two. I was very happy when Edward Taylor, the music critic of the Sheffield Telegraph, wrote 'Peter Glossop is making his debut in the production and we shall watch his career with interest. He almost stole the show.'

After this success, Eva Rich gave me the lead baritone roles in her next two productions of musicals with the Teachers Operatic Society of Sheffield – the Prince in *Waltz Time*, and

D'Artagnan in *The Three Musketeers*. In the meantime, lessons with Mrs Rich continued. One day, not long after I had appeared in the production of *Waltz Time*, I was waiting outside her room for my lesson when I heard a beautiful mezzo-soprano voice inside the room singing the Habanera from Bizet's *Carmen*. I was due to start at three o'clock and normally if the previous lesson was running over time I would not dream of barging in, but this time immediately the clock struck three I felt an uncontrollable compulsion to do just that. That wonderfully musical voice had attracted me like a magnet.

When I went in I saw a ravishingly beautiful black-haired girl leaning on the piano and looking at me languidly. I went completely weak at the knees and there and then fell in love. I excused myself to Eva Rich by explaining that I just had to see the owner of the voice I had just been hearing, so she introduced us. The young lady then left and Eva immediately told me that her pupil was working in order to pay for her lessons and I was not to imagine she was free for any romantic attachment as she was devoted to her singing! I never did find out exactly how that possibility got into her head right then, but it was an ironic statement because four years later Joyce Blackham was to become my wife.

It wasn't just this young lady's looks, it was also her voice that captivated me – it was incredible for a seventeen-year-old. She had already been singing concerts for four years and she had a marvellously mature sound and style. Our relationship actually started when we both sang in *The Three Musketeers* with Eva Rich's company. At the first rehearsal I heard loud chattering behind me and looking round I saw this beautiful girl. 'Excuse me' I said 'Aren't you the girl I met in Eva's studio?' 'Yes' she said. After that I didn't pay much attention to the rehearsals as I was more interested in talking with Joyce. I discovered that when I had first met her she had already seen me in *Waltz Time* and now that I was singing the part of D'Artagnan, she had joined the chorus in the hope that we might meet again. Very soon we were seeing each other as boy and girl friend and at every possible opportunity when we were both not on stage singing we would wait for each other under the stage and have a cuddle.

One night in *The Three Musketeers* I had my first taste of what can so easily happen in a theatre performance. There is a scene with a sword-fight and unknown to me I just caught the edge of my opponent's nose with my sword. He suddenly came at me in a real rage and I genuinely had to defend myself. At the end of the scene I realised something was very wrong so I ran away as quickly as I could but he caught up with me behind the stage and tried to attack me. I still did not know what this was all about and when he accused me of injuring him I was flabbergasted and tried to tell him I had no idea that anything had happened. That was to no avail at all because he just went berserk. I imagine the scene on stage must have come over particularly convincingly that night.

My next operas with the Sheffield Singers Opera Society were Thomas's *Mignon* in which I sang Lothario and Verdi's *Ernani* in which I took the part of the King, Don Carlo. *Ernani* was a very ambitious undertaking indeed for an amateur company as the four principal roles are particularly demanding and had I known beforehand how famously challenging the part of Don Carlo is for baritones I would probably have been very nervous. As it was I had no idea about its reputation, so I sailed through it without fear and received rave notices. With all this I was quickly becoming well known in Sheffield because I was soon engaged to sing in concert performances of operas alongside established singers from London who were brought up for the events. This is how I sang my first di Luna in Verdi's *Il trovatore*, Valentin in Gounod's *Faust* and Amonasro in Verdi's *Aida*.

I felt I could have a professional future as a singer so I applied to take part in the Great Caruso Opera Competition which was being organized by the Hollywood film industry to boost their new star Mario Lanza. In England the auditions were divided up geographically into several areas and the North section was held in Leeds. I sang the Prologue from *I Pagliacci* and was awarded the regional prize and a place in the national final in London, which was to be held in April 1952. Before the final I made a trip to London to audition for the chorus of the Sadlers Wells Opera and so now I sang the Prologue again, this time on the stage of Sadlers Wells Theatre for my audition. Judging me was the Administrator of the Company, Norman Tucker.

After I had finished, a member of staff came up to me and said the Administrator would like a word with me. I went into the stalls and was welcomed by Mr Tucker who asked me what my goal was. I replied 'My ambition is to sing Rigoletto on the professional stage.' I also told him I was just about to sing an audition for the Covent Garden Opera Company chorus too. He chuckled and said 'At Covent Garden a chorister is in the chorus for life, but at Sadlers Wells if our young choristers merit it we make them Principals.' That was enough to decide the issue for me. I would go to Sadlers Wells, even though in no way at this moment could either Norman Tucker or I have possibly known that in seven years time I would indeed be singing the title role of Rigoletto on the stage of the Sadlers Wells Opera. Nothing like that could possibly happen today. Back in the 1950s the Sadlers Wells Company consciously looked for potential Principals who might be in the chorus and someone like myself with no professional experience to date could only hope for the chance of becoming a Principal by joining the chorus first. By the 1970s all that had changed and on the whole young Principals were being engaged as company members from outside, either as already established performers or as new young soloists. With only a few exceptions, singing in the chorus was no longer a possible route to becoming a Principal.

I received a contract for the Sadlers Wells Chorus just a few days after my audition, but with the Caruso competition final only a fortnight away I waited before signing it as the first prize was a year's tuition at the La Scala Opera House in Milan. So I travelled to London again and after the preliminary round of singing I was chosen as one of the six finalists. The national final itself was to be broadcast on BBC radio. At the eleventh hour the BBC realized that in a thirty-minute programme there was only room for pieces by five singers and so the organizers of the competition decided to draw lots to choose the five and lay off one unlucky finalist – who turned out to be me. I was extremely upset, but the following day I was in the company manager's office at Sadlers Wells signing my contract. I was to start in the chorus in August of that year, 1952, at the start of the company's new season. I did not know where it was going to lead at the time, but my great adventure was about to begin.

CHAPTER TWO

Sadlers Wells – The Journey Begins

I left Sheffield for London in early August 1952. I had no knowledge of the city at all, as I had only been down a very few times on quick visits. It seemed a far away place in those days and although I was excited at the prospect of joining a major opera company, in the weeks running up to my departure it was also daunting to realize that I was going to have to go and live somewhere in a huge city where I would be a complete stranger. However, by a stroke of luck, a close friend of my uncle Arthur had been visiting his relatives in Sheffield in June. His name was Tom Evans and fifteen years earlier he had left Sheffield for London to start his career as a violinist. He was now a member of the BBC Concert Orchestra. When he learned that I was going to be joining Sadlers Wells with no knowledge of London and no idea where I might live he immediately offered to find a flat for me. He was as good as his word and when the time came to leave Sheffield in August I made my way to the designated flat in Priory Road, Hornsey. With me came my sister Doreen as she didn't want to be left behind in Sheffield. We were pleased with our ground floor flat, even though it only had one bedroom, which Doreen had. I bought a bed settee and took the living room. I also bought a rather battered piano, which was essential so that I could accompany myself during my voice practice. Above us

Books from frass

Your feedback is appreciated.
If you have any complaints etc
then please contact me at:
  janmcochrane@yahoo.co.uk

To search or browse through
our other books visit
  www.amazon.co.uk/shops/frass

Thanks for your custom

1a Greystones Avenue, Sheffield S11 7AY

on the first floor were two elderly sisters who owned the property.

Doreen started looking for a job at once and very quickly found a position as a secretary with the Canadian Black Label Lager company that was just starting up in England. From that she earned fifty per cent more than my income at the time! But I loved my new life from the very beginning. The first day that I walked through the stage door of the Sadlers Wells Theatre I felt a thrill – I was a professional and was earning my living from singing, and I was going to show everyone what I could do. I was bellicose in those days if I wanted something, although at the time I had no wild dreams about being an international star. Right then, for me it was wonderful to be singing in the chorus of a real professional company and, remembering what Norman Tucker had told me, who knows I might even be offered a principal role later on. If that were to happen at Sadlers Wells I would be very excited, because the company's reputation was constantly growing.

When Lilian Baylis had founded the Sadlers Wells Opera before the Second World War it was the first permanent opera company in London. When Norman Tucker was appointed Director in 1948, with his acute ear and knowledge of music he embellished what Lilian Baylis had established. He built up a superb ensemble of very talented people and boldly expanded the repertoire, bringing the Company a special prestige. He gave it an identity of its own that was quite different from the Covent Garden Opera Company that the brilliant David Webster had founded in 1946. That great organisation was later to become one of the most celebrated and magnificent of all opera companies and I was to have some of the most memorable experiences of my life singing there as a member.

When I joined the Wells in 1952, opera was sung in English

all the time at Sadlers Wells and most of the time at Covent Garden, but whereas Webster was already beginning to lead the Garden on to an international route with more operas performed in the original language and star guests such as Kirsten Flagstad, Maria Callas and Boris Christoff, Tucker was building something very different at the Wells. Like Webster, he was fielding fine new singers, but they performed a different repertoire in which the Company formed a highly distinctive style. There certainly were the great European masterworks, but there was also a commitment to new and less well-known opera. Back in 1945 the Company had given the now celebrated première of Britten's *Peter Grimes*, and during Norman Tucker's eighteen years as Director, from 1948 to 1966, there were acclaimed new productions of, at the time, rarely heard operas by Respighi, Janáček, Bartok, Stravinsky and Delius, and many contemporary English composers such as Lennox Berkeley, John Gardner and Richard Rodney Bennett. Many of the stagings were imaginative and very well rehearsed, and the days of massive interference by directors with concept productions that departed radically from the composers' and librettists' intentions were thankfully quite a long way in the future. For London audiences, Sadlers Wells and Covent Garden complemented each other effectively, and especially so after the mid 1950s when Covent Garden became a fully-fledged international company performing nearly all its repertoire in the original language.

My first impression of the Sadlers Wells chorus was that more than half of them were Welsh. I was right, as I was soon told by one of them 'You do realize this is Sadlers Welsh Company, don't you?' It was a very good chorus and the atmosphere was friendly, although there was one Bill Smith who took me aside and pointed to one of his colleagues and said 'You see him over there. He's no good. We only get him in here as a booster.' I said 'What's a booster?' 'He's there to make the others sound better than they are,' he shouted. When the Welsh fought with each other they went at it hammer and tongs, but it was really only friendly fighting, so to speak.

Most of the chorus were certainly very supportive to me and helped me learn my new profession as I went along. At the first full stage and costume rehearsal, which was for the first opera of the season, a new production of *Samson and Delilah* by Saint-Saëns, one of them said 'Where's your make-up?' 'What make-up?' I said. 'Your make-up for the stage!' 'Well then, you tell me, where is it?' 'You do it yourself, didn't you know?' I hadn't realized that in the chorus there is no longer the luxury of having a make-up lady as there had been when I sang the principal parts with the amateur companies in Sheffield. So I had to borrow some make-up from one of the choristers until the next day when I went out and bought a make-up box for the first time in my life. I learned bit by bit, but always with the help of my colleagues – throughout my first three months or so one of them always checked to see if my make-up was acceptable. After that I was all right on my own. I also had to learn the new discipline of singing in a chorus when your performance had to match that of your colleagues as exactly as possible. Very early on, the chorus master came up to me and said 'Peter, when you get to the front of the stage, could you cut it down by half, because all we can hear is you!' A back-handed compliment, I suppose.

From the beginning of my time at Sadlers Wells I felt that virtually the entire company was a happy and devoted group, with people wanting to help each other. What a contrast from how everything had become three decades later, when so much personal ambition and greed was by then the driving force, as it also became with most other opera companies in my experience. Back in the 1950s we were like a family and as such our careers were nurtured. I spent one whole year in the chorus and during that time I was given two small cover parts, that is understudying two principal roles for a possible performance if the principal singer is ill and cannot go on stage. Although I never did have the opportunity to sing them in a performance, this was an important opportunity to find out how I might be able to manage a principal role.

My new friends in the chorus recommended that I contact Appleton Moore to have lessons. He was a retired professional bass-baritone and he was an expert on the vocal technique of the baritone voice, including the old Italian *bel canto* school, which was to prove to be very valuable for later years. Unfortunately, he could not play the piano and it is absolutely essential that a singing teacher can accompany the pupil on the piano and also play while he or she demonstrates anything vocally. Occasionally he brought in a lady pianist, but she could not play very well and frankly gave me more problems than benefit in my lessons. Such is the vital importance of a singing teacher who can play the piano! At the end of my first year I felt I had to find another teacher.

Meanwhile, we had opened the 1952 season at Sadlers Wells in September with the new production of *Samson and Delilah*, followed by several revivals and then a new production of Verdi's *La traviata*. One of the performances was on 5 December, which was the first day that the great 'pea-souper' smog covered London. The lethal mixture of fog and smoke was so heavy that it practically brought the city to a standstill. Visibility was down to less than six feet and I had to struggle to walk to the Underground station, which was running fairly well as it was under the ground. I managed to arrive at the theatre just in time for curtain up to find a shambles. The smog had drifted right inside, and even with all the extra lighting brought in by the technicians we could not see the conductor properly and the performance quickly fell apart. It was abandoned after the first act. I later learned that all the audience could see was a brightly lit fog.

After the performance I managed to get home again safely, but I was coughing severely all the way. That evening thousands of people all over London gave up trying to find their way home and spent the night in doorways and bus shelters. The next day many elderly people were found dead from the cold and damage to their lungs. The smog lasted another three days. It led to the government eventually bringing in a law that only smokeless fuel could be used in Greater London, to prevent a future disaster.

During my first year at Sadlers Wells there were two music directors – James Robertson and Michael Mudie. Michael Mudie, who was very highly regarded, fell seriously ill and had to leave before the end of the season. During the year quite a number of productions he was scheduled to conduct were instead taken over by a brilliant young Australian musician who was quickly coming into prominence as a conductor with great theatrical flair and a real command of all the complex technical elements in opera. Charles Mackerras had first been engaged as a repetiteur and coach at Sadlers Wells in 1947 and he also sometimes played the oboe in the orchestra. In 1948 he made a strong impression as a dynamic and disciplined conductor when he took over a run of performances of *Die Fledermaus*, by Johann Strauss, with virtually no rehearsals. The year before I joined the Company, in 1951, he had introduced the music of Janáček, which was virtually unknown to operatic audiences in England and little known outside

Czechoslovakia at that time. His idiomatic performances of *Katya Kabanova* were a major watershed for Janáček, Sadlers Wells and himself, and he was to become the world's most admired authority and interpreter of this composer's works. He was also excellent in everything else that he conducted, which was a very wide range of operas indeed. He was demanding but practical and unfailingly obtained first-class results. More than fifty years later he is still flourishing and is surely one of the most versatile and erudite of all conductors.

As Norman Tucker had promised, in the spring of 1953 we choristers were all given the opportunity of singing a solo audition on the stage for the management. This had a twofold purpose: firstly to hear if any of the older singers were getting past it and secondly to hear if any younger singers were developing. I sang Silvio's aria from *I Pagliacci*, both because I didn't think it had been sung well during the season and also, especially, because it finishes on a top G, which is a speciality of mine. The singer who had been performing Silvio was mediocre, if that, and every time he almost suffocated on the top G. The result of my rendition was that I was immediately raised to the rank of Principal for the next season, along with a great friend of mine who had joined the chorus on the same day that I did. He was the Scottish bass David Ward, who was later to become internationally acclaimed as a performer of Verdi and Wagner roles. For both of us, this decision by Norman Tucker was the most vital step up the ladder in our lives.

*   *   *

In August 1953, the Sadlers Wells Company reconvened to prepare for the new season. My sister and I had by now found a new apartment overlooking the River Thames in Richmond.

My first Principal rôle at Sadlers Wells – Morales in Carmen, 1953

The opening opera was *Carmen* and for my first principal role I was given the small part of the officer Morales, who sings in the first act only. It is indeed only a very small appearance, but many of the reviewers singled me out and here I was at the very beginning of my career as a soloist in the Company receiving very good notices for a minor contribution. I did feel proud. Soon after, I was given the role of Prince Yamadori in Puccini's *Madam Butterfly* and the Marquis d'Obigny in *La traviata*. These were also small roles, but vital in giving me the opportunity to feel my way as a new Principal. Additionally I was made an understudy for the role of Schaunard in Puccini's *La Bohème*, so I had plenty of coaching. This was very important for me as I had never received any formal musical education, as distinct from voice lessons. In my coaching sessions I sapped up everything I could and I continued to learn in that way throughout my career. No matter how successful or experienced an opera singer is, there is always something new to learn and I was very fortunate that both at Sadlers Wells and then later at the Royal Opera House Covent Garden I had the benefit of working with outstanding teams of musical repetiteurs who were highly knowledgeable about the styles and details of the operas and also aware of the many dangerous places where there could be pitfalls in performance. Sadly, teams like that have long vanished from both opera houses.

In the 1950s most of the productions at Sadlers Wells were straightforward and generally in keeping with the original instructions of the composer and the librettist. Some were imaginative and some were not so good, but there were as yet few if any of the so-called concept productions that were to dominate this company, in particular much later when it was the English National Opera. It was in the 1960s that a trend to updating and reconsidering the characters' personalities and functions in operas began in many parts of the world. By the 1980s these concept productions, often blatantly altering the intentions and sentiments of the original operas, had become more frequent occurrences in most major companies, but nowhere more so than at the English National Opera. Whereas in many opera houses they were forays into experimentation, at the ENO they became central company policy and, for me, increasingly obliterated the meaning and truth of the works they purported to reinterpret for contemporary audiences.

In recent years, some of these pretentious and misguided productions have made complete nonsense of the great masterworks of composers such as Mozart and Verdi, notably the ENO stagings of *Don Giovanni* and *Un ballo in maschera*. I do not accept in any way that having toilets on the stage in *Un ballo in maschera* enlightens a twenty-first century audience who can supposedly relate better to this than they can to a traditional staging observing all the details that Giuseppe Verdi and Antonio Somma so meticulously indicated. And that is just a detail in a production that, like so many at ENO and also elsewhere, decided on radical changes to the actual characters in the opera. Even when for the première of *Ballo* Verdi himself had to change the period and place from eighteenth century Sweden to seventeenth century America to quell the authorities' fears of possible subversion because of a staging featuring the assassination of a king, the original essence of the characters – their feelings and their social positions – were maintained. In his many battles with censors, Verdi never countenanced any interference with the original concept and sentiment of his operas. He was draconian about that and one wonders just to what lengths he would go to deal with the ENO if he were alive now and saw their production of *Ballo*.

During my first season as a Principal at Sadlers Wells, Joyce Blackham and I were married. At the time I joined the Wells in 1952, Joyce's father had arranged that she sing for his managing director, who was on the Rotherham City Council, so that she might obtain a grant to enable her to study at the Guildhall School of Music in London. She succeeded and was the first ever singer to receive a music grant from Rotherham. So, three months after I left Sheffield, Joyce followed me to London and by this time we were engaged. I had to fight for her, though. In January 1953 I was ill in bed with influenza and Joyce came to see me, but not with a tonic. She told me that she was having a wonderful time with the other students at the Guildhall and wanted to be free. She broke off the engagement and gave me the ring back. I was devastated although hardly surprised. All the men at the Guildhall were chasing her, she was so stunning. But I had a feeling that if I bided my time she might come back to me, so I waited seven months and then, in August 1953, I contacted her. To my delight she agreed to see me again. A few months later we were holding hands during a performance of *La traviata* at Covent Garden and in the second interval she allowed me to replace her engagement ring. A year thence, on 8 January 1955, we were married at Marylebone Register Office. It was one week after Joyce's twenty-first birthday, I was twenty-six, and both of us were on the way to exciting operatic careers.

Not so long into my first season as a Principal at Sadlers Wells I began understudying a larger role, Nourabad the High Priest, in a new production of Bizet's *The Pearl Fishers*. Shortly before the performance was due to take place I was informed I had to go on stage and sing the part as David Ward, who had been cast in the role, was sick. So now this was the first time that I was performing a leading operatic role at Sadlers Wells and in fact I sang far better than I had done in any of the smaller parts before. This was an important experience, because immediately I knew that I was much more comfortable and confident in a major role. From the moment I went up on stage I felt completely in control and authoritative as the high priest who has tight command over all his subjects. I knew straight away that at that moment I was absolutely this person as an actor as well as a singer.

Incidentally, the real reason that David Ward, a wonderful singer, had been taken 'sick' was that the previous night he had gone up to his home country of Scotland for a wedding and during the proceedings had become paralytically drunk. I am sure he would not mind my recalling this now, because we were good friends and had a strong mutual admiration. Our

With Joyce Blackham around the time of our engagement

lives developed in parallel in many ways as we both joined the Sadlers Wells chorus at the same time and we both developed our careers at Sadlers Wells and then the Royal Opera House fairly simultaneously. We were also both known for being provocatively irreverent on a number of occasions! David became one of the world's very finest basses and many people feel his Wotan in Wagner's *Ring Cycle* has never been surpassed.

The Pearl Fishers is of course nothing like as popular as *Carmen*, but for a young composer of twenty-five it is a remarkable achievement. The great Act 1 duet alone, 'Au fond du temple saint', as Zurga and Nadir meet in the temple and swear they will not be rivals over the beautiful Leila, is one of the most magical moments in all music and is one of the world's most famous compositions. The role of Nourabad is not at all spectacular, but he expresses his power and authority through recitative and denunciation, and as I had a larger voice than average I was able to make something out of this and create a dynamic impression. My performances received extremely enthusiastic notices and from then on my career was really on the up.

The very next day I had a telephone call from Joan Ingpen of the music agency Ingpen and Williams. She had seen my performance and felt I was just the artist she was looking for to sing duets in a film with the Maltese tenor Oreste Kirkop. He had a wonderful voice and Hollywood had already snatched him up for his first film, a musical, which was just about to be released. I was now asked to sing with him in his second movie. Joan Ingpen warned me that when a decision to record was made I would have to fly out to Hollywood at very short notice. So I waited, and in the meantime the first film came out. When the telephone call finally came it was to tell me that

Oreste Kirkop had pocketed his large fee and gone back to Malta. He disliked Hollywood and there was nothing the directors could do to persuade him to return. With the money from his film he bought himself a fishing boat for the beach life in Malta, which was all he wanted. So that was that. I was almost, but not quite, in a Hollywood movie.

At this time I began to sing roles with the Fenna Opera Concerts, a small group who gave concert versions of operas with piano accompaniment. In due course this seemingly modest activity was to prove of considerable significance for the development of my future. We played small theatres and concert halls that were easily accessible from London and over several years we performed operas such as *La traviata, Faust, Rigoletto, The Barber of Seville, Die Fledermaus* and *Don Pasquale* – all invaluable experience. When in 1956 the society ceased to exist because the founder manager became seriously ill, the singers and I took it over and we formed a new company called The London Opera Group. I arranged the casting and the operas and we enlarged our team of singers, which now included my wife. Within the restrictions of concert performances we concentrated as much as we could on acting the operas and we began to build a considerable demand for our performances, which also began to attract the interest of the critics. Anything happening like that today would be unimaginable. Young singers now do not spend years and years learning their roles and gradually building their careers even in major companies, let alone local music societies. Those with the greatest talent are bred and conditioned for competitions and if they succeed they are performing big roles all over the world very soon afterwards. More about that later!

At the beginning of the 1954/5 season I started to have

lessons with Joseph Hislop, the celebrated Scottish tenor who had enjoyed a prestigious career. Although I was now becoming well known and the future looked very bright, I felt it was essential to continue studying and especially with a fellow professional, as when it comes to teaching, the value of a performer's practical experience can never be matched by a theoretician. The reason it was Hislop I went to was to do with my fiancée. He had already been a strong influence on her singing and he thought very highly of her. She had spoken to him about me and in any case he was already familiar with my work because he was on the Sadlers Wells Board of Directors. It was in fact Joseph Hislop who interested Sadlers Wells in Joyce. While she was a student, Hislop had heard her sing Rosina in *The Barber of Seville* and he was so impressed that he recommended Sadlers Wells hear her and then take her on board. So Joyce actually never auditioned for the Company. Quite exceptionally they invited her to join when she had finished her studies, which she did in January 1955, becoming Sadlers Wells's youngest ever Principal at just twenty-one years old. It was the start of what became a brilliantly successful international career.

During the next couple of years at Sadlers Wells I sang an extremely wide range of repertoire and increasingly the Company cast me in larger roles. A big step forward was Schaunard in *La Bohème* as this is much more than just a cameo part such as I had mainly been playing up to then. Although Mimi and Rodolfo are the big stars of the opera, Marcello, Colline, Schaunard and Musetta are all important character roles within the entire drama. In Schaunard I had an opportunity to sing and act in equal proportions, which is absolutely how I had always wanted to perform in opera. Another important role was Silvio in *I Pagliacci*, a lyrical part that contrasts strongly with the jealous and very dramatic character of Canio who finally finds out that it is Silvio with whom his wife Nedda has been having an affair. When I was cast as Silvio I was particularly happy because singing the malicious Tonio in the production was my favourite baritone in the Company, Frederick Sharp. I was already deeply committed to the music of Verdi, and Sharp was my ideal Verdi baritone. He had the exemplary combination of perfect dark colour with high notes and he was a fine actor – all the essential qualities for performing Verdi's baritone roles. He was altogether the major baritone at Sadlers Wells in those early years of mine there. I was amused when I was told that after our run of performances of *I Pagliacci* Fred had been astounded that every night I had taken the optional high A instead of the written C in the duet with Nedda. He had said in his broadest Yorkshire dialect 'If he doos that I give him six moonths!'

Even amongst high baritones, as opposed to the deeper bass baritones, there have never been that many singers who have felt safe with very high notes such as a top A. I was fortunate to have a naturally wide vocal range, but I had also been expertly taught a special technique to solidify the voice and additionally give it maximum flexibility. It was in fact Appleton Moore who had developed in me the pharyngal voice, which is a mixture of the head and chest voices, but with much more of the head voice and the aperture almost closed, almost like humming. It is the traditional, Italian *bel canto* way of singing *mezza voce*, literally 'half voice', and it enables a baritone to float smoothly and securely when he has to go up to a pianissimo E natural, which is the worst note in his compass. It was really rare for an English singing teacher of the time to have the capacity to pass this technique on to a pupil, but Appleton Moore had mastered it.

As I said earlier, I had to leave Mr Moore after a year because he could not provide a decent piano accompaniment, which is essential for singing lessons. When I then eventually went to Joseph Hislop, he developed and refined my technique in other ways. His teaching had been criticised in some quarters, but he felt especially able to help me because I was already an experienced professional and he felt he could give me something that would be wasted on many of his other pupils. With his different expertise coming after Appleton Moore's I was able to develop a really strong and resourceful vocal technique over a period of time. This is so essential for a singer, which sounds obvious enough, but then history has shown that many performers have not really formed a sufficiently secure technique in the formative years of their careers and in time they encounter difficulties that can become catastrophic. And those formative years extend a long way beyond just the beginnings of their professional lives.

In January 1956 I played my first Masetto in Mozart's *Don Giovanni*. One reviewer said 'Peter Glossop was more like a peasant from deepest Surrey than from old Seville.' A great start to the year, but fortunately I didn't get many notices like that. The rest of the season proceeded along not dissimilar lines to before with a large number of supporting and also smaller roles, but then in early 1957 something important happened. It was decided that I would understudy a fine Polish baritone, Alfred Orda, in the role of Count di Luna in *Il trovatore,* as Sadlers Wells was to open its new production of the opera on its spring tour (each year the Company toured the provinces of England for twelve weeks from around the end of March). Later in the season I would have the opportunity to sing a few performances on stage. This was a major new opportunity and a big step forward as di Luna is one of the most ambitious of all Verdi's baritone roles and it requires great reserves of colour and strength as well as a masterly technique and powerful stage presence. I knew that my future would depend on how I coped with it.

As it turned out, not for the last time in my life was I to benefit from a stroke of theatrical fate. Two weeks before the first night of *Il trovatore* I was called to see Norman Tucker, who then told me that Orda had walked out of the rehearsals and resigned his role. The part of di Luna was now mine. Far from being apprehensive, I was thrilled. Fortunately I had already sung the opera in a concert performance in Sheffield three years earlier and I knew it very well. The first night opened the spring tour on 25 March, in Newcastle, and it was a wonderful experience. All the cast – Victoria Elliot, Ronald Dowd, Sheila Rex, Harold Blackburn and myself – were enthusiastically received and I felt at last that I had begun my new career as a true Verdi baritone. I also felt that I really could project a major dramatic role, the likes of which I had not yet had the opportunity to perform on stage. Remembering Caruso's famous dictum that '*Il Trovatore* is an easy opera to cast – all you need are the four greatest voices in the world', I was at last certain that I would be singing all the great Verdi baritone roles in due course.

I mentioned how, as has been the case with many singers and actors, fate on a number of occasions gave me vital opportunities when I had to stand in for another artist at the last moment. Now though, whilst I was enjoying the most exciting successes of my career so far, fate was to bring a year of unforeseen tragedy to my family. After living in a small flat in North London, in 1956 Joyce and I had managed to save enough money to buy our first house, in East Barnet. In early 1957, not that long before the *Il trovatore* performances, Joyce became pregnant and was not too pleased about it because she had intended to move further ahead in her operatic career before starting a family. As time progressed, though, of course the baby became the priority in our lives.

As we neared the time of the birth we ordered a fancy pram and I booked Joyce into Barnet General Hospital. On 1 June I took Joyce to the hospital in the early morning and then left her with the staff, as I had a full day's rehearsing at Sadlers Wells. When I arrived back at the hospital in the late afternoon, on announcing my name to the nurse on duty she immediately said 'Would you come with me, Sir, the Matron would like to see you.' This alarmed me but it did not begin to prepare me for what was to follow. 'I have very bad news,' the Matron said. 'Your wife was delivered of a baby girl late this afternoon. The baby seemed to be well and healthy and was shown to your wife, who heard her cry. The two nurses put the child aside and tended to the mother. After thirty minutes, one of the nurses returned to the baby and noticed she had stopped breathing. They immediately called the surgeon but it was too late. Your daughter had died of anoxia – a failure of the lungs. Nobody has yet informed your wife. Do you wish me to tell her or do you wish to tell her yourself?' I replied that I would do it.

My wife was still in the delivery room. When she saw me, she cried out 'What's happened, Peter? They have taken my baby away and I want to hold her! Has something gone wrong?' I had the heartbreaking task of telling her what the Matron had told me. We just broke down and wept and wept.

Joyce had to stay in hospital for a week after the birth as she was very weak. I fetched her home on 8 June and had to carry her to her car and then into the house. I went back to the shop to inform them that I no longer needed the pram I had ordered. The lady in the shop told me that when I had said that my wife was booked into Barnet General Hospital she had grave misgivings. She told me she had more cancelled prams from births at that hospital than any other. I later learned that the mortality rate of births at Barnet was double that of any other hospital.

Somehow Joyce and I found the strength to carry on and I continued with the Sadlers Wells summer tour. Our summer holidays were spent in our home so that Joyce could begin to recuperate. But it was a long haul for her as she was very weak and everything she had been through had resulted in the loss of her capacity to sing – a terrible added blow (it was to prove temporary, but at the time we could not know this). At the start of the new opera season she was nowhere near ready to begin performing again. So while I went back to sing at the Wells, she remained at home. And now, on top of all this began another intensely traumatic period that was to end in another dreadful tragedy.

When we had bought our house in East Barnet, my mother had sold her Sheffield house to help Joyce and me find the extra money we needed, over and above the money that we had saved up. The idea was that she would have her own room in our home, in perpetuity. Unfortunately this arrangement began to become very difficult indeed as mother would bring home bottles of her favourite sherry and lock herself in her room with them. Then she would descend on the kitchen at midnight for her supper and some music.

Increasingly life became nightmarish, as mother would drink herself into a great stupor and become extremely vociferous. In the seventh month of Joyce's pregnancy, my mother went up to Sheffield to be with my sister for a short time, but very shortly after we had lost our baby she came down again to live with us. The reasons for this are too complicated to list here, but suffice it to say that after all we had been through and with Joyce now weak, shaken and totally unable to sing, it just became impossible to have mother staying with us in her condition which was becoming worse by the day. Joyce loved my mother and got on very well with her, but the situation was threatening her recovery – seriously. I had to put the recuperation of my wife above everything else and so I explained the predicament to my mother and she volunteered to find other accommodation. Both Joyce and I were terribly distressed that this had to happen, but we had no alternative for the sake of Joyce's health.

My mother found a small flat in Sussex Gardens, in the Paddington area of London, and I helped her to move in. That day she said to me 'When your father died, I promised myself that I would look after you children, which I have done. I lost your elder brother when he was sixteen, but I have seen you and your sister become established in your lives. Now you don't need me any more and I want to go to your father.' I did not pay sufficient attention to her words. Two weeks later a policeman knocked at my door to tell me that my mother had been found dead in her flat. Her head was in the gas oven.

I had my mother cremated and then took the ashes to Sheffield, where she was finally reunited with her husband and eldest son, in our family grave. And still, our tragedies were not over. Some years later Joyce's and my second child was stillborn. We never did have children together. My offspring were to come from my second wife, much later.

*   *   *

It was because of the success of my performances of di Luna in *Il trovatore* that Sadlers Wells now began to cast me regularly in major roles. In early 1958, whilst I was still trying to come to terms with my mother's suicide, I sang my first Germont père in *La traviata*. Then, the following year, for the first time on stage I tackled two parts that I have greatly loved ever since: the title roles in Tchaikovsky's *Eugene Onegin* and Verdi's *Rigoletto*. When the original production of *Eugene Onegin* had first been performed at Sadlers Wells, the stage director and conductor had both been Russians, and their concept had in many ways been continued by George Devine, who had created a new production in 1954. That is one reason why I was cast as Onegin, because I was very much a dramatic baritone and in those days at the Bolshoi Theatre the roles of Onegin and Tatyana were always sung by the Company's leading dramatic baritones and sopranos. In Western theatres, it has often been the practice to cast them as lyrical baritones and light sopranos and whenever I have heard them performed like that I have simply felt that the production teams have not known what the composer had in mind. Tchaikovsky did specifically say that he wanted *Eugene Onegin* to be a series of intimate, lyrical scenes, but that does not mean that he wanted light voices all the way through. There are such intensely passionate moments in this masterpiece and the singers need to be able to convey them with great emotional power.

For me, this opera is as much a tragedy about the clash of understanding between classes as it is about the failings of Eugene Onegin. I see Onegin as a lost man with a split personality and not just the self-centred, cold-hearted cad that he seems to be right up until the last two scenes of the opera. As a young Russian aristocrat in the early nineteenth century, he is very defensive of his rank in society and he considers all the people at Madam Larina's country estate beneath his station. He only comes to pay them a visit because of Lensky, who is his closest friend. After the dreamily romantic Tatyana meets him there and falls deeply in love with him, he genuinely disdains her for writing a letter pouring out her heart to him. He feels he is above that kind of thing, as you might say. Of course that does not in the least bit excuse the insensitive and patronising way he speaks to her, nor his appalling behaviour at the party when he flirts with Lensky's fiancée and provokes Lensky to challenge him to a duel. By then it is too late to make amends, not that he really wants to, and so Onegin ends up killing Lensky, as he fires first in the duel. Despite all that, I don't think that Onegin is just callous. For me he is sick, and it is his music in the first two acts that tells me this. Beneath that indifference and nonchalance there is a trace of frustration and bitterness as though he maybe could be capable of genuine passion instead of just being cynical and hopelessly bored all the time. In the last act, when he comes back after five years' absence and sees how Tatyana is now a poised and alluring young woman, he does fall violently in love with her and goes to her on his bended knee. It is far too late, as she is now married to Prince Gremin, who is much older than her, and even though she does still feel her passion for Onegin it is inconceivable that she will suddenly abandon her marriage and run off with him because his feelings have changed. 'I am loved by an honourable man,' she tells Onegin, 'and I have a duty to him.' And so this time, after a few minutes together, it is Onegin who is rebuffed – and broken.

One interpretation is that Onegin's behaviour in this last act only reinforces what a monstrously selfish person he is, but that is not how I see him. I think that it is only now that for the first time he fully realises what has been wrong with him and he desperately wants to try and mend the dreadful mistakes he has made. True, he was not expecting to see Tatyana again and he has suddenly been swept off his feet by her, but also after

*Eugene Onegin, with Ava June as Tatyana, Sadlers Wells, 1962
(by kind permission of Donald Southern and the English
National Opera Archives)*

five years he has known sorrow, he has suffered and he is full of genuine remorse. Now he truly is a human being, speaking with his heart to Tatyana. At the very end of the opera his final top G is a deep cry of anguish. It is much more than just the pain of heartbreak. It is the despair of a man's recognition that he has ruined his life and the lives of others.

I strongly feel that Onegin is a tragic character rather than a bad man. He is a victim as much of his background as of his own personality. And that is underlined by the way that after Tatyana has moved up into the aristocracy and assumed an even higher rank than his, he finds his feelings towards her change dramatically as he sees her sophistication and allure. It is not her new status but her new poise that so strongly affects him. But the cruel irony is that in the meantime he has also changed and now in his honest fervour of love he truly realises far too late that he should never have behaved in the way he did before. I empathise with him in one respect – I have never stopped regretting that I was divorced by my beloved first wife, Joyce, but my wisdom and repentance came much too late to restore our marriage. I am more fortunate than Onegin, though. Tatyana bids him farewell for ever, but after subsequent marriages and divorces Joyce and I are now close friends again.

Hot on the heels of *Eugene Onegin* came a revival of *Rigoletto* and my first stage performance in the title role. I won't discuss the part here, because it is one of the great Verdi roles I cover in the chapter on Verdi later on, but I will just say that it is one of the most vocally and psychologically strenuous of all operatic parts. Despite that, for my debut I was going to have minimal rehearsal because the opening night was to be on tour and there were several other operas that also had to be prepared. It was now that my experiences with the London Opera Group really showed their value, because one of the operas we had performed in a semi-staged concert version was *Rigoletto*, and that had been my very first experience singing the role.

Rigoletto opened in Stratford-upon-Avon on 19 March 1959. It felt a momentous occasion as this was the role I had always wanted to sing above all others ever since I had first seen the Carl Rosa Company on their visit to Sheffield. Unfortunately, this first night was an unhappy anti-climax. The theatre had a very dry acoustic, which made a heavy night's singing, and I was not at all satisfied with my performance. It was not until the next week when we played the Lyceum Theatre in my home town of Sheffield that at last I felt I had begun to achieve my goal. From that day onwards I felt a particularly strong conviction with Rigoletto on stage and it was indeed to become one of my most famous roles.

The next season at Sadlers Wells opened with a big new production by Anthony Besch of Giordano's *Andrea Chenier*, with Charles Craig as Chenier, Victoria Elliot as Maddalena and myself as Gerard. The success of this brought me an important opening: EMI records invited me to make my first recording, singing the role of Essex in Edward German's *Merrie England*. Everything was looking rosier all the time, but it was not long before I had to endure one of my earliest battles in the theatre.

My next new major role was assigned to me later that season, in the spring of 1960. Norman Tucker had invited the stage director Denis Arundel to mount an ambitious new production of Puccini's *Tosca* at Sadlers Wells, with Colin Davis, the recently appointed Music Director, conducting. Marie Collier was cast as Tosca, Charles Craig was Cavaradossi and I was Scarpia. From the very first rehearsal I could sense that Arundel didn't approve of my presence. It wasn't long before we clashed over quite a number of details and then Arundel admitted that he had from the start tried to prevent my being cast as Scarpia because he said I was too young. He told me he was going to see Norman Tucker to 'protest' me – an operatic term for refusing to work with an artist. I went home devastated and had a very depressing weekend. On the Monday morning Mr Tucker called me and asked if I would go and see him straight away. When I arrived, to my surprise he told me that he had firmly instructed Mr Arundel that I could not be replaced under any circumstances. So, I was able to sing my first Scarpia after all. I wonder how many opera intendants of today would be so loyal to a house artist in the face of pressure from a celebrity director.

I see Scarpia as a monster with virtually no redeeming features. Mind you, the extent of his evil is as much in his position as it is in himself. The supreme power he enjoys enables him to go far further than he otherwise could. But at the same time he is an extremely powerful personality in the way he unfalteringly calculates everything he does. When I play him, the only time he ever betrays genuine passion is when he starts to go for Tosca. He really is bowled over by her and at first he could almost be capable of showing feeling. But his real strength, in the perverse sense, then comes out when she repulses him. He is viciously ruthless and his entire plan to exploit her is not in the slightest bit affected – until she suddenly stabs him, that is! The three most malicious characters I know of in opera are Scarpia, Iago and Claggart, but in a sense Scarpia is the most sadistic of them all in that he enjoys the way he twists and tortures people. With Iago and Claggart there are sinister, dark jealousies and disturbances that motivate them towards a specific person in the most complex ways. That doesn't redeem them at all, but I think Scarpia operates on a different psychological level.

My performances of Scarpia brought me some of the best success of my career so far, although there were some critics who were unfavourable towards my interpretation. Contrast *London America* 'the masterful Scarpia of Peter Glossop . . . dominates Act 2, infusing the cat-and-mouse game with the heroine with suffocating tension' with the *Financial Times* 'Mr Glossop's Scarpia was in a curious way unconvincing . . . Perhaps it again held too much suggestion of lessons carefully learned, but the result not yet brought to life in a performance.' Interestingly, both the *Financial Times* and *Daily Mail* reviewers seemed to be concerned with what they felt was under-statement. 'He sang with distinction, but it is also the voice of a gentleman, and it seemed to me that its honesty went some way towards killing the character. Scarpia is a gentleman, as we say, but of monstrous and permeating nastiness. Glossop was polished, but, notwithstanding all his efforts, not odious enough.' An artist should not answer his critics, but I do feel I should say here that these reviews bring up the whole issue of how far you should go in making a character look and sound overtly evil if you are to be really convincing.

I had one more new role that season, Wolfram in *Tannhäuser*, my first Wagnerian part. More about that in the next chapter on the Royal Opera House, Covent Garden, for a reason that will become evident then.

*   *   *

The following year, 1961, I was approached by the Handel Opera Society to sing the role of Argante in Handel's *Rinaldo*. The rehearsals and performances were to take place in Sadlers Wells Theatre while the Wells company was finishing its tour and starting its summer holiday, so I was able to accept the engagement, which was to include three further performances in Halle, Handel's birthplace. It was the first time I had sung any music by Handel and I must say I had to condition myself very carefully after having now spent many years performing nineteenth century opera and especially Italian opera. As it turned out, I much enjoyed the music and the role, but the most memorable part of the occasion was the discovery of a remarkable new talent. A young woman began her first aria and I was so impressed with the beautiful quality of her mezzo soprano that when she finished and came down into the stalls I said to her 'I think you have a really lovely voice and you sing so musically. I think you have a very fine career ahead of you. Would you mind telling me your name?' 'Janet Baker,' she replied. Soon she was to become one of the world's most sought-after artists.

During that year, a notice appeared on the information board at Sadlers Wells Theatre giving details of an opera competition that was to take place in Sofia, Bulgaria. It was called The International Young Singers Opera Competition and it immediately caught my interest. The age limit was thirty-three and as my thirty-third birthday was to take place during the actual dates of the competition, I was just eligible to take part. All competitors had to pay their own air fares to and from Sofia, and although a Yorkshireman doesn't like spending his money without knowing he is going to get something for it, I decided to go. One reason for this was that for the very first time in the Competition's history, the final round was to be a performance with the Bulgarian National Opera on the stage of the Sofia Opera. Before that, though, I would have to qualify through the first two rounds.

For round one I sang *Silent Noon* by Vaughan Williams. That put me into round two, which was held in the Sofia Concert Hall. The public was seated on the ground floor but the members of the jury, who included the celebrated soprano Toti del Monte, were in the balcony behind a curtain, where they

The Sofia competition, 1961, with my Russian accompanist

could hear but not see the competitors, to ensure there was no nationalistic partisanship. I began with the Count's aria from Mozart's *The Marriage of Figaro*, which I then followed with the Prologue from *I Pagliacci*. For the *verismo* of the Prologue I felt free to indulge in a touch of theatre. I loosened my tie and took off my jacket, placing it on a chair nearby. That caused some murmuring from the public and I later learned that the jury members, who of course could not see anything, were dying to know what was going on. At the end of the Prologue I gave everyone a long high A flat, followed by an even longer G in the very last phrase – and I was through to the final round on the stage of the Sofia Opera.

The opera to be performed now was *Il trovatore* and I was to sing the role of di Luna. There was only the minimum of rehearsal and then the curtain went up on the performance with a Bulgarian tenor singing Manrico in Italian, a Bulgarian soprano singing Leonore in Bulgarian, a Polish mezzo soprano singing Azucena in Polish and an English baritone singing di Luna in English. This multilingual performance of Verdi's great opera resulted in my winning the gold award jointly with the Bulgarian baritone, Assem Selimski, and consequently invitations to sing in many countries in the then communist Eastern bloc. They were my first engagements by continental opera houses, and although I am so critical of the way competitions dominate the fortunes of young singers today, I have to confess that this one was very beneficial for the start of my international reputation.

On my return to London I went straight into rehearsals of Britten's *A Midsummer Night's Dream* in the role of Demetrius. This was a production by the English Opera Group but it was being incorporated into the Covent Garden Opera Company's visit to the Edinburgh Festival in August. As such it was to be my very first performance with the Company. After the first night there was a party and to my surprise the General Administrator, David Webster, came up to me and asked if he could have a word with me. We went into a quiet corner and he asked me what kind of contract I was on at Sadlers Wells. I explained that I had just recently signed a new two-year contract. He then said 'Would you please promise me now that you will not sign another contract with Sadlers Wells before coming to see me first?' I was happy to say that I would promise. It was perhaps the most significant moment for my international future.

Near the start of the 1961/1962 season at Sadlers Wells I took part in a revival of *Rigoletto* and an incident occurred that, looking back on it now, is just one example of how greatly the world of opera has changed since then. The conductor was

James Lockhart, with whom I was singing for the first time. During the final rehearsals, in Act 2 he complained about my shaking the bells on my jester's stick before my entry into the court. This is a wonderful moment as it heralds Rigoletto's approach to the scene where all the court, except Rigoletto, knows that the Duke has just gone to seduce his daughter. As Marullo sees him arrive he says 'Poor Rigoletto'. When the dress rehearsal came I was staggered to find that the bells on my bauble had all been cut off. After the rehearsal was over, I immediately went to the wardrobe department and insisted they give me the bells and the bauble. I took them home with me and sewed all the bells back on the bauble. On the first night I made my customary ringing of the bells to announce my arrival to the court.

The next morning I had a telephone call requesting I see Mr Tucker in his office. When I went to see him, to my amazement he reprimanded me telling me I had behaved badly and must apologise to Mr Lockhart. I immediately said 'But I had the approval for my action from the stage producer who surely had the authority for this.' This was completely true, as I had carefully checked with him before sewing the bells back on to the bauble. 'Maybe you did,' said Mr Tucker, 'but in the opera house the final decision in any argument lies with the conductor, who can override any difference he may have with the stage director or designer.' Needless to say, I apologised as ordered. Years later, when I was singing *Don Giovanni* in Hamburg with James Lockhart conducting, he would always say before the performance 'Don't forget – no bells on your bauble' and we always laughed. Now – can you imagine anything like that situation happening today? Very few if any conductors can overrule a stage director any more. Sometimes they walk out after disagreements, as do directors too, but they are now rarely able to enforce their wishes solely through their position.

In December, the English Opera Group's *A Midsummer Night's Dream* transferred to the stage of the Royal Opera House Covent Garden and for the first time I sang in that great, legendary theatre, taking the role of Demetrius as I had in the summer tour. Actually Covent Garden was too large for the intimate atmosphere of this work, which is really a chamber opera, but for me it still did not spoil the wonderful atmosphere. I have a special love of this opera, even though my role is not anything special. Britten brings such a magical sound into the woodlands. Later I was to have the great privilege of performing with the composer himself, both in concert and opera. I have always loved his music and consider him one of the last great operatic geniuses.

1962 marked the tenth anniversary of my joining the Sadlers Wells Opera. I was so happy there and yet I could not forget that wonderfully unexpected exchange with David Webster the previous summer in Edinburgh when he had asked me to come and see him before I sign another contract with the Company. Although it would, on the face of it, have to be the best part of two years before this could happen, I was already imagining with great excitement what it might be like to sing at the Royal Opera House more regularly.

No matter how excellent it was to be with the Wells, which was such a fine national company, there was a halo around the name Covent Garden Opera Company, for under Webster's remarkable leadership it had by then become one of the most internationally prestigious of all opera houses and for the last four years it had been enjoying unprecedented success. The memory was still fresh of what became a legendary production of Verdi's *Don Carlos*, in 1958, with the fabulous cast of Jon

Vickers, Tito Gobbi, Gre Brouwenstein, Fedora Barbieri and Boris Christoff singing with the acclaimed team of Carlo Maria Giulini conducting and Luchino Visconti producing – a watershed in post-war opera in England. Maria Callas had been appearing at the Royal Opera House as Norma and Violetta in some of the most special events in memory, Joan Sutherland had created a sensation in the title role of *Lucia di Lammermoor*, Otto Klemperer had made a tremendously impressive debut conducting *Fidelio* at the tender age of seventy-five – and so on and so on.

Covent Garden had glamour, frisson and, above all, the highest standards and so the approach from Webster had made an impact on me. But even then, I could not have forecast that I was to have my first major international opportunity there within just a few months and that I would be singing a role in an opera by the composer that I already loved over and above all the others – Verdi. In the event, for all the awe of such a sudden jump, the transition was to feel remarkably smooth and natural.

CHAPTER THREE

Going to the Garden

Fairly early in my career at Sadlers Wells, the Company and I had realised that I was very fortunate to have a natural feel and vocal make-up to sing the baritone roles of Giuseppe Verdi. As I will explain later, there are very specific qualities that are vital for a Verdi performance and I believe it is true to say that there has always been a relative shortage of truly suitable Verdi singers, and that includes Italian artists. In particular, news of my performances of Rigoletto and di Luna at Sadlers Wells had spread beyond the confines of the Company and so it was that not long after my encounter with David Webster in Edinburgh in the summer of 1961 I was summoned by Norman Tucker. He told me that the Covent Garden Opera Company had asked Sadler Wells if I could be released from my contract so that I could be a reserve standby for the role of Renato in a production of Verdi's *Un ballo in maschera* the following March, with the opportunity to sing just one performance, the last of the run, on stage. In those days there was a gentlemanly understanding between Sadlers Wells and Covent Garden and Norman Tucker realised this was a very important opportunity for me, so it was now up to me whether I wanted to take up the offer. Of course I did.

I was to be the 'cover' for the celebrated Ettore Bastianini, the reigning baritone king of Italy at the time, and my one performance would effectively be my Covent Garden Opera Company début, since my previous appearances at the Royal Opera House had been with the English Opera Group. It was going to be a tremendous challenge to follow Bastianini and sing in Italian with an international cast for the first time, and so immediately I was offered the contract I enrolled at the Berlitz School and began having Italian language lessons. I had never sung in Italian before and did not even speak the language so I worked like a slave. Fortunately I was also given invaluable advanced Italian tuition as part of the most thorough possible coaching in the musical and dramatic elements of performance by the Covent Garden music staff. This was at a time when the company's repetiteurs were recognised as amongst the very finest in the world. They were fluent linguists and highly informed musicians and it was the Covent Garden policy to give singers long and extended periods of pre-rehearsal preparation with them. Amongst them I particularly valued Edward (now Sir Edward) Downes and John Matheson, who were such a fountain of wisdom and vitally helped so many singers, and I made the most of this opportunity by asking for as many coaching sessions as possible. This I was granted and I never felt happier than when setting off to Covent Garden many a time to prepare for the great role of Renato.

Daunting as the challenge of making my Covent Garden Opera Company début seemed, I soon found out that the atmosphere at Covent Garden at that time was as happy and friendly as it was at Sadlers Wells. The big international stars felt this when they came as guests and on the whole they and the resident members integrated like a family – quite unlike how everything later became. Perhaps jealousy has something to do with it, but today there is not the binding together that is the core of all opera and indeed all theatre performance. This is vital so that each role and every performer can interrelate as they should. Back in 1962 there was a wonderful spirit of ensemble at Covent Garden and it extended to newcomers like myself as well, artistically and personally. The support that new artists felt from their colleagues and from the music staff was a major help towards that extra special confidence one needs for an important début.

The big night finally arrived on 12 March 1962. With the excellent preparation I had received and the knowledge that the Covent Garden Opera Company was behind me, I felt I could hold my own with anybody. In the first act of *Un ballo in maschera*, Renato has one aria, not a particularly special or popular one, but when I finished it I had a round of applause. This had never happened in the previous performances with Bastianini and it instantly gave me a great surge of confidence. I knew I was in good voice and so when Renato's great, defiant aria 'Eri tu' came I felt I could give it all my reserves of power and feeling. At the end the audience gave me a wonderful reception and I really felt I had arrived where I belonged, on the stage of an international opera house singing Verdi.

I must mention here that in preparing for this performance of *Un ballo in maschera* I had my first meeting with the great tenor Jon Vickers who was singing the role of Riccardo (or King Gustavus the First in Verdi's original nomenclature). We immediately felt a special rapport. We both shared the belief that acting is as important as singing in opera and this single performance of *Ballo* was the beginning of a twenty-year partnership singing together all over the world. I especially cherish the memory of our many performances at La Scala Opera House in Milan. We also recorded and appeared in filmed opera productions together, mutually enjoying many

Amonasro in Aida, *Szeged, 1962*

memorable triumphs. To this day we remain firm and great
friends.

The *Ballo* performance was so successful that the Covent
Garden management immediately engaged me to sing two
more Verdi roles – Amonasro in *Aida* and Germont in *La
traviata*. These performances were scheduled for September
and November 1962 respectively and they were to be the first
of more and more invitations to sing at the Royal Opera
House – and not just in Verdi operas. Although I was still on
contract with Sadlers Wells, Norman Tucker recognized the
direction that my life was taking and he gladly allowed me to

accept all the Covent Garden offers so that in the autumn of 1962 I was singing in *Aida*, *La traviata* and *La Bohème* at Covent Garden, and *Rigoletto* and *Tosca* with Sadlers Wells on tour – quite some commuting.

There was never any trace of hostility or reservation about my appearing with both companies. Nobody at Covent Garden tried to put me down in any way and nobody at Sadlers Wells resented my new success at the big international house across the other side of the city. I wonder if such a broadminded attitude would exist today when singers are far more viewed as being suitable mainly for one or other kind of opera house. It was the same with the press. After my first performance as Amonasro, with a cast of Anita Valkki as Aida, Charles Craig as Radames and Fiorenza Cossotto as Amneris, Leslie Ayre in the *Evening Standard* wrote 'The new boy in the cast was Peter Glossop from Sadlers Wells singing his first Amonasro. He gave us genuine baritone quality and in return I give him my compliments.' Frank Granville Barker in *Music and Musicians* wrote 'The newcomer among the men was Peter Glossop, who gave an assured and aristocratic performance as Amonasro. It was his dramatic fervour that brought the opera to life for the first time – in the Nile scene – and vocally too his was an extremely successful assumption of the role.'

Just five days later I sang Marcello in *La Bohème* at Covent Garden for the first time, with the wonderful Renata Scotto as Mimi, and once again the press drew attention kindly to my presence at the Royal Opera House as a visitor from Sadlers Wells. In the *Daily Express*, the critic Clive Barnes wrote 'It was a pleasure to find the young Sadlers Wells baritone, Peter Glossop, making his Covent Garden début as Marcello. His voice was still not consistently well-focused; when it is he will become a baritone of international stature.' It was this kind of notice and the enthusiasm of the Covent Garden audiences that led Norman Tucker to call me to come and see him at the beginning of 1963. He told me that David Webster had been speaking with him and had asked if Sadlers Wells was prepared to transfer my contract, which still had several months left to run, to Covent Garden as in fact I was at this time giving more performances there than I was at the Wells. 'There is no point in us keeping you here when Covent Garden needs you,' he said, 'so I am giving your contract to Mr Webster. I don't want to stop your international career. But please come back and sing for us when you can.' It was a demonstration of the remarkable gentlemanly relationship that existed between the intendants of Sadlers Wells and Covent Garden at that time. And so it was that I now became a member of the Covent Garden Opera Company – and reciprocally, they allowed me to guest at Sadlers Wells as well; indeed I was also allowed to sing in many other places.

When I look at my diary of 1963 I am amazed I managed to fulfil all that I had taken on. At Covent Garden I sang in two more runs of *Aida*, four further runs of *La Bohème*, a new production of Wagner's *Lohengrin* (taking the small but exposed part of a Herald), a series of performances of Verdi's *Don Carlos* in which I was Rodrigo, a run of *I Pagliacci* in which I took the role of Silvio and two series of performances of Puccini's *Turandot* in which I was Ping. Meanwhile at Sadlers Wells I had a further series of performances of *Rigoletto* plus several appearances in Henze's *Boulevard Solitude* singing Lescaut. In Glasgow I sang my first Iago in Verdi's *Otello*, with Scottish Opera. I was in Plovdiv (Bulgaria) in *Rigoletto*, *La traviata* and *Tosca*, in Hungary at the Szeged Festival with *Il trovatore*, and in Edinburgh and Zurich singing in *A Midsummer Night's Dream* with the English Opera Group. I also sang in Berlioz's *Leilo* at the Edinburgh Festival, Bartok's *Cantata Profana* at a BBC Promenade Concert and a selection of operatic extracts in a memorable recital with Benjamin Britten, Peter Pears and Galina Vishnevskaya at the Aldeburgh Festival. And with all this I was also understudying some further parts at Covent Garden, one of which was to have a very fateful outcome the following year – more about that later.

My first new role on contract at Covent Garden was Ping in *Turandot*, which I was hard at work rehearsing in between appearing in a series of performances of *Rigoletto* at Sadlers Wells. Ping is not a big part and most of the singing is in little trios with the other two ministers of the Chinese court, Pang and Pong. It may seem surprising that I was putting in such a lot of time to a small role but this is the important responsibility of a singer of a comprimario character. I sang few of these little subsidiary kinds of parts as Covent Garden were mainly casting me in major principal roles, but those that I did perform I took every bit as seriously as the big dramatic characters. In the best operas, comprimario roles are usually vital in their minor ways and there is a special art in their performance. In *Turandot*, Ping, Pang and Pong bring a humane balance, as does the slave girl Liu, to the extremes of the icy Princess Turandot, the obsessed Prince Calaf and the sadistic court.

I even collected a brief compliment for my performance of Ping from Frank Granville Barker in *Music and Musicians*, as I did from several reviewers when I performed another even smaller role several weeks later. That was in a new production of *Lohengrin* by Josef Gielen with a wonderful cast and the great Otto Klemperer conducting. Sandor Konya sang Lohengrin, Régine Crespin was Elsa, Rota Gorr was Ortrud and Covent Garden company members John Shaw and David Ward sang

Telramund and King Henry respectively. I was cast as the Herald, and now I am going to indulge myself and quote one critic's comment about my contribution because I feel his words proclaim the importance of the comprimario: 'In the part of the Herald, Peter Glossop was in tremendous voice. He looked and sounded authoritative, his voice rang through the theatre like the trumpet calls that announce the Herald's utterances, and he convincingly showed us why this part, though comparatively short, becomes a leading one when interpreted by an artist of stature.'

This was my first experience singing in German and, as I had done with the Italian language, I had spent a great deal of time working very hard on the pronunciation. Now that I was singing at Covent Garden I had to perform in many languages and this was soon to prove a major asset for the development of my international career. As for Dr Klemperer, he was a man to esteem. Although he was nearly seventy-eight years old and had for the previous twenty-five years or so been afflicted with appalling bouts of ill health, paralysis and accidents that would have destroyed many people half his age, his concentration was intense and his talent was blazing. There was absolutely no doubt whatsoever about what he wanted and, with only a few words, he absolutely had his way. I felt I was taking part in history singing in his *Lohengrin* performances.

Looking back, it seems now that almost every production I took part in during my first season on contract at Covent Garden was a special event. The new cast of *Aida* in April featured three big star guests, Galina Vishnevskaya in the title role, Regina Resnik as Amneris and Joao Gibin as Radames, with Michael Langdon, Victor Godfrey and myself from the company taking the roles of Ramfis, the King and Amonasro. Hot on its heels was another run of *La Bohème*, this time with

Sena Jurinac as Mimi, Alain Vanzo as Rodolfo, Adele Leigh as Musetta and myself as Marcello. It was company policy to put guest artists and regular contract members together on stage and for the company members like myself the opportunity to sing with such distinguished guests added an extra frisson to what was already a very exciting atmosphere at the Royal Opera House.

The Covent Garden Opera was now hugely admired world-wide and everyone knew that its enviable record of achievements was the progeny of its founder and General Administrator David Webster (later to become Sir David). He was greatly respected and revered at the House and he cut a formidable and, on the face of it, remote figure. He had true authority and did not attempt to mingle informally as became the manner with most of the later intendants, but he could be disarming all the same. We used to have singer with piano rehearsals in the building opposite the Royal Opera House stage door, which was known as 'No 45' (the address was 45 Floral Street), and the entrance to David Webster's office was just a few paces away from one of the studios in the same building. One day, a group of singers, myself included, were chatting away outside this studio while we were waiting for it to be vacated for our rehearsal, when Sir David came down the corridor. All of a sudden we were all silent – totally silent. As he walked towards us he nodded and then just as he had passed us he turned round with 'And f— you too.' It was wonderful to know that our revered Sir David Webster had a marvellous sense of humour.

On the whole one did not see much of David Webster, but his influence could be felt by all of us. We knew we had a gem of a leader and, just as with my previous gem of an employer at Sadlers Wells, Norman Tucker, I knew I was receiving the best possible help in my prime, because neither man had any favourites and they were concerned to nurture the careers of their singers in the best and most sensible ways both for the artists and the opera houses. At Covent Garden the artists had great confidence in Sir David. We trusted him and we knew he would look after us. I do not believe there has been anything like that since his time. It has all become so very different, with opera houses functioning much more as bureaucratic, impersonal promoters rather than developers of talent. I am far from the first to say this, but I feel it needs to be reiterated. It was by no means all a bed of roses before, and I for one felt that the Music Director Georg Solti was excessively authoritarian and inflexible, but the outstanding feature of Covent Garden when I was a member was its commitment to its artists and the astuteness with which its staff put that into operation. It was Sir David Webster's caring and brilliant leadership that was responsible for all this.

21 September 1963 was the date of another revival of Puccini's *La Bohème*. Singing opposite Joan Carlyle's Mimi was a very gifted young Italian who was making his début at the Royal Opera House. Immediately I heard him at our first rehearsals I said 'this is a lovely lyric tenor'. He was to become perhaps the most widely successful opera singer of the twentieth century, even including Enrico Caruso and Maria Callas. Our new Rodolfo was Luciano Pavarotti, and he and I immediately got on very well indeed. He sang beautifully, so it is quite amusing to look back at the reviews for what is now that historic first night. Frank Granville Barker in *Music and Musicians* mauled it, writing 'Abysmally lighted, the stage picture was a disgrace to an international house, and though rehearser John Copley had clearly tried to give it some life, the action was feebly handled.' Leslie Ayre wrote in the *Evening*

News 'It introduces to us a new and very pleasing young Italian tenor, twenty-seven-year-old Luciano Pavarotti, as Rodolfo. This is not a huge voice but it is sweetly lyrical and Mr Pavarotti pays us the compliment of really singing in tune. Joan Carlyle's touching and nicely sung Mimi teams up with him to make a credible pair of young lovers. Peter Glossop's Marcello is splendidly sung, with genuine Italian-type baritone quality throughout the range.' Well, I think in all modesty I seem to have come away best there, and yet Frank Granville Barker differed from Leslie Ayre when he said 'Her (sc. Elizabeth Vaughan singing Musetta) Marcello, Peter Glossop, was robust in character, though he sang far too loudly most of the time. His is a glorious voice, however, and he could make the ideal Marcello.'

So often I read reviews of the same performance where some critics say you have not enough voice for your part and others say you are too loud. I wonder if it has something to do with where they are sitting in the auditorium. Even then, the location of a seat cannot explain the kind of extreme difference in reaction that was given to the *Aida* revival back in April. In *Opera*, Percy Cater wrote 'The Vishnevskaya voice is a brilliant instrument. Singing seems to cost the Russian prima donna no effort. And the liquid sound – so enchanting to the ear and the mind – now tender and heart-appealing, now surging to thrilling force, is partnered by an actress's instinct of a fine and rare sort.' Now here is Frank Granville Barker in *Music and Musicians*: 'Resnik was always the Princess, never turning to vulgarity for emphasis: even in the second act duet with Aida she kept her violence under control while her bearing in the Triumph Scene was truly regal. Resnik was a tower of strength in ensembles and deservedly received the biggest ovation of the evening. In complete contrast to Resnik, Galina Vishnevskaya presented the character of Aida as a composite of the Vamp of Baghdad and a take-off of Theda Bara.' As they used to say – 'You pays your money and you takes your choice.'

To be fair to the critics, although Pavarotti sang so splendidly in his *La Bohème* début, it was impossible then to foresee that in a few years time he would be one of the most sought-after superstars in the history of opera – back in 1963 one thought of heroic tenors, in the tradition of Caruso, as the very biggest names. But the more I sang with him the more I admired the absolute precision of his voice placing. I feel the only other tenor of the last few decades who has been equal to Pavarotti in this respect is Jose Carreras. Both of them had this magnificent focus in their voices, and had Carreras not fallen so terribly ill I am sure he would have continued to sing as he did in his late twenties, in the way that Pavarotti has continued to amaze audiences whilst he is in his sixties. If you have this kind of focus you can go on singing for most of your life. Happily Jose has made a remarkable recovery after nearly being struck down totally by leukaemia and he has managed to recapture some of that wonderful quality of his earlier days. He and Luciano do differ in one respect though: Luciano does not really act – he concentrates purely on tone and line. And that is another reason why his voice is so extraordinarily well preserved. In my own case I also had a true focus in my voice, but I felt it did not matter if I had to tear myself to pieces to make a character like Scarpia really shake the theatre and make the audience cringe as he should.

Pavarotti is unique, though, and he has always sung so very beautifully. He and I became good friends during his first weeks at Covent Garden and I took him to a number of my favourite Italian restaurants in London, especially the La Scala just opposite the Royal Opera House where, needless to say, he loved the food. Although he was a much slimmer young man at that time he could already put his food away like a champion.

After the first three performances of *La Bohème* we had a cast change and I had the opportunity to sing with the great and legendary Giuseppe di Stefano who was of course taking the role of Rodolfo. Sadly he was out of form and it would be unfair to report a critic's view under these circumstances. Only another singer understands the awful position of having to perform a big role knowing one is not in voice but must nevertheless stay the course to the end, at whatever cost. As it happened, on this occasion I received some of the most complimentary notices of my time at Covent Garden so far, with *The Observer* even saying 'Mr Glossop, indeed, emerging as the star of the show.' I mention this only to illustrate how the fortunes of one's career can be affected by a performance of a role that is not necessarily considered the 'star' part of the evening. Just as the small comprimario parts are so very important as I said before, in the finest operas the more secondary principal roles are in their own way as vital as the big title characters. In *La Bohème* Rodolfo and Mimi sing the most famous arias in the first act, but it is Puccini's portrayal of the relationships between all four Bohemians, Mimi and Musetta, all so different and yet, as the opera's tragic finale so heart-breakingly substantiates, inseparable, that is the essence of this wonderful work.

I have already mentioned the outstanding team of repetiteurs who were resident at Covent Garden at this time, and at this point I must pay tribute to the late Maurits Sillem who was a really marvellous coach for *La Bohème*. Quite apart from his enormously wide-ranging knowledge, he was a deeply intellectual man and this was particularly valuable when it came to the music of Puccini. That may at first sound surprising in view of the emotionalism in Puccini, but on the contrary he offered the most wonderfully discerning and aware insights into the composer's works. I soaked every session up with him, just as I did with Ted Downes, the most magnificent teacher of Verdi in my experience and also a conductor of rare stature in that composer's works. Of all the conductors of Verdi operas that I performed with I felt the two very finest were Sir Edward Downes and Carlo Maria Giulini. With repetiteurs like Sillem, Downes and also the French music expert John Matheson at hand, I was avaricious for coaching sessions – which is not at all how one has so often felt about going for lessons! These were very special musicians in their own right and they were pouring out new ideas.

There was another name on the Covent Garden music staff that was later to become famous, although not at the Royal Opera House. I had in fact first come across him when I was at Sadlers Wells and was sent to him for coaching when I was singing Wolfram in Wagner's *Tannhäuser*. By now you may have guessed that this was Reginald Goodall. He was largely ignored as a conductor at Covent Garden, for a variety of reasons that I will not go into here, and he only began to make a real name for himself after the Sadlers Wells Opera engaged him to conduct Wagner's *Die Meistersinger von Nürnberg* in 1968. That created something of a sensation and he then went on to lead a new production of the complete *Ring Cycle* of Wagner, one of the most important and successful English language performances in operatic history. But long before all that, Reggie was greatly admired by international singers as a source of fantastic knowledge and understanding of the operas of Wagner and although he now hardly ever conducted at Covent Garden he remained on the music staff as a Wagner coach almost up to the end of his life in 1990.

When I was at the Wells, Goodall occasionally guest conducted and he was engaged to be in charge of a revival of
Tannhäuser on a ten week tour in 1960. He always required a
great deal of preliminary preparation with each and every
singer, so well in advance of the first scheduled rehearsals
I went to his small room at Covent Garden up in the amphitheatre, which everyone called 'Valhalla', and had my first
coaching sessions with him. They were a revelation. This
strangely shy and seemingly diffident little man was a spring of
inspiration and a tower of strength. He had a profound understanding of the meaning of every note and word of the opera,
and never allowed any fault to pass, no matter how transient it
might appear. I remember so vividly how he enlightened me
when we reached the moment in Act 2 when Wolfram delivers
his tribute to Elisabeth at the contest of love songs. Previously
I had always sung this aria gently and when I began Reggie said
'What's wrong? Aren't you singing in full voice today?' I said
I was continuing the mood of beauty and repose set by the
orchestra as Wolfram slowly walks to the podium and prepares
to play his harp. 'No,' Reggie said 'the music we have just
played has nothing to do with the song you are about to sing. It
denotes the nobility of Wolfram's heart and informs the public
who you are. When you start the song, it should be strong and
ardent as Wolfram has a heroic character.' I suddenly realised
that after all the performances I had been giving of Wolfram
before at Sadlers Wells I had never understood my role. I
am sorry to say that I don't think the conductor of those
performances, James Robertson, had ever understood it either.

For me it was a great loss that Goodall was neglected at
Covent Garden. After his triumph at Sadlers Wells he did
conduct Wagner's *Parsifal* and then Beethoven's *Fidelio* at the
Garden, with Jon Vickers in both productions, but those apart

he was hardly ever on the podium there after the 1950s. As I said before, there were many reasons for this and David Webster, who in fact admired him considerably, understandably had his concerns, which were reinforced when Georg Solti became the Music Director. Sir Georg once said at a press conference that he felt Goodall was no longer capable of conducting a complete opera at Covent Garden. For my part, I much preferred Goodall's Wagner to Solti's, which was diametrically opposite in concept. There are certain passages in Wagner's music where you do want that virility that Solti brought, but the real feeling and animation and above all the tragedy in the score came through with Goodall. He conducted the text, and the musical contours and colours came out of the words, whereas I always felt that Solti was just conducting the musical score. Reggie put a lot of extra time on to every performance with his slow tempi, but it was sheer heaven. We always thought, both at Covent Garden and at Sadlers Wells, that when Reg Goodall conducted Wagner, the hand of Wagner was on his shoulders.

After the revival of *La Bohème* came my next and, in many ways, most challenging role so far at the Royal Opera House. I was cast as Rodrigo, the Marquis of Posa, in Verdi's great opera *Don Carlos*. The production was the famous Luchino Visconti staging that had been such a landmark for Covent Garden when Carlo Maria Giulini had made his House début with it conducting a fabulous cast five years earlier. *Don Carlos* is a beautiful opera, one of Verdi's very finest, and Posa is a great and noble figure with wonderful music to sing, so I was very eager to perform him, not least because I could not have found a greater contrast to the many villains I had been singing in my career up to then. It is generally much harder to play a saint than a villain, so I felt particularly keyed up for my début in this part.

Rodrigo in Don Carlos, *Royal Opera House, Covent Garden, 1968*

The new cast was also highly prestigious, with the great Bulgarian bass Nicolai Ghiaurov as King Philip the Second, Gre Brouwenstein as Elisabeth of Valois, as in the 1958 première, Ragnar Ulfung singing Don Carlos, Fiorenza Cossoto in the role of Princess Eboli and David Ward as the Grand Inquisitor, with myself as Posa. Edward Downes conducted. The opening night was on 4 October and with a cast like this the success of the performance was assured, however I have to single out Nicolai

Ghiaurov. His great voice rang through the House and thrilled everyone. I have always regarded him as the world's greatest bass of his generation and I am proud that he and I have been great friends ever since these performances. I collected even more enthusiastic notices than I had received up to then at Covent Garden. They were nearly all substantially detailed in their praise and this performance of Posa became my biggest success so far. The opera was always a special favourite of mine for the rest of my career.

During the performances of *Don Carlos* I received a letter from the management of Covent Garden regarding the renewal of my contract, which was due to expire in July 1964. They offered me £80 per week, which was a nice increase from the £50 I was getting from the Sadlers Wells contract that had been taken over by the Garden. I now remembered how after the Di Stefano performance of *La Bohème* two months earlier, the tenor's agent Sandor Gorlinsky had come to see me in my dressing room and told me that if ever I wished to have the help of an agent for my career he would be more than happy to represent me. I had never had an agent and so I said I would bear that in mind, but now that the Garden was offering me an increase to £80 it seemed to me that I did not need any representation, so out of courtesy I phoned Gorlinsky to explain the position. I did say to him though that if he thought he could negotiate an even higher increase he would certainly be earning his ten per cent commission. He said 'leave it with me'. The same day he called me back to say he had discussed the matter with David Webster and Sir David had agreed to pay me £120 a week. So, even after paying ten per cent to Gorlinsky, I was £28 a week better off. I was over the moon and immediately made Sandor my personal agent. He was to serve me well throughout my career.

In that month of November 1963 a new production of *Il trovatore* was being planned for the following year at Covent Garden. David Webster had already engaged Carlo Maria Giulini to conduct the opera and he suggested to the Maestro that I should sing the role of Di Luna. Giulini came to hear me and said he was happy with my voice but would like me to study the language and pronunciation in finer detail in Italy. So, it was agreed that I would be given a month's tuition in Modena with Leone Magiera, who happened to be Luciano Pavarotti's accompanist. I was delighted that Covent Garden were prepared to provide this for me and it particularly pleased me that I would be going to study with Maestro Magiera in Modena, as this was Luciano's home town and he and I had become very good friends. So, on 23 November, two days after the last *Don Carlos* performance at Covent Garden, I drove to Modena and arrived there on the 25th. A hotel room had been arranged and I began lessons the following day.

When I was free I spent a lot of time with Luciano, who was at home without engagements during my month in Modena. One day he took me to his father Fernando's bakery for lunch where we had Fernando's freshly baked bread, a huge plateful of Parma ham, which was a local speciality, and a few bottles of the local wine, Lambrusco. A simpler meal it was impossible to have, but it was of absolutely superb quality and years later we were to recall the memory many times.

Luciano and I appeared together quite a bit in those days and we really did enjoy a very good friendship. Before long he became incredibly famous and yet he always remained friendly to me. Very many years later, when we were appearing together in *Tosca* at the New York Metropolitan Opera, we got into the same lift with a white-haired old man. 'Do you remember my father?' Luciano asked. Of course I did, even though it must have been the best part of twenty years since that wonderful meal at Fernando's bakery. We shared some happy memories and Luciano was, as he always was with me, full of fun. But now I do have to say that back in the mid-1960s I saw a huge change in him when he shot to stardom. There was a two year gap when we didn't see each other and then when we met again I felt he had become grand in his manner, bragging about the famous aristocrats who were now his friends and admirers. He developed an ego about himself that he never had before, and part of this took the form of a 'prima donna' attitude at rehearsals and a growing inclination to cancel performances. This is such a pity because I remember Pavarotti as such a simple, straightforward lad in the early days. I think he felt that as he became a superstar, it was expected of him that he would behave in the way that he did. Fortunately, this never affected the quality of his singing one bit. To this day he has always sung beautifully, a wonderful artist.

Maestro Giulini had asked that I sing to him again after the month of tuition in Modena and so after a final supper with Luciano, his wife Adua and his two daughters (later there were to be two more) in Luciano's apartment, the following day I took the train to Rome, where it had been arranged that Giulini would hear me. He was conducting Verdi's *Falstaff* at the Rome Opera House and he had requested I sing for him on the stage there after a rehearsal. When I arrived in Rome I telephoned Gabriele D'Averio, a local agent who worked with Gorlinsky and who had recently obtained an engagement for the fine English tenor Charles Craig to sing Radames in *Aida* at the Caracalla Opera. We met the next day and he was present when I sang for Giulini in the Rome Opera House. I felt I had sung well and Giulini said he was now happy with my pronunciation and would be writing to Covent Garden with his decision.

Although he was so demanding he gave me a wonderful feeling of confidence, which I was to value so greatly when I sang di Luna in the *Il trovatore* performances at Covent Garden the following November.

As Gabriele and I left the Rome Opera House, Gabriele said he had a surprise for me. He took me to the headquarters of the Italian Radio and Television Company (RAI) where, unknown to me, he had arranged another audition. I duly sang some items from my repertoire for the RAI panel and afterwards Gabriele said he was sure that my début in Italy would more likely be in a radio concert than in a theatre. He was to be proved correct and this was the start of a twenty-year collaboration between us in which he became a staunch and true friend and helped me enormously in Italy. It was also to be the beginning of a love affair with Italy where I was to enjoy some of my most rewarding artistic times and experience undreamed of successes – but more about that later. For now, the most dramatic event in my career was just about to come around the corner back in London at Covent Garden, although at this moment I could not possibly have foreseen it.

CHAPTER FOUR

Covent Garden – Gateway to the World

There are some remarkable instances in history when a performer's international fame has suddenly been made by stepping in to replace somebody else at the eleventh hour. Arturo Toscanini made his sensational conducting début in *Aida* with literally no notice at all when the audience in Rio de Janeiro refused to allow the assistant conductor of the touring opera company, of which Toscanini was an orchestral member, to mount the podium because he was replacing their local conductor who had stepped down after a dispute. Leonard Bernstein shot to fame when he replaced an ailing Bruno Walter and conducted his New York Philharmonic Orchestra concert at several hours' notice. Tito Gobbi sang his first big role with a major opera company at one day's notice when he was a last minute replacement for Père Germont in a production of *La traviata* at the Teatro Adriano in Rome and he was instantaneously acclaimed. I can think of quite a number of other artists who became celebrated after they had been thrown in at the deep end and, with all due modesty, I was one of them. In this instance, though, I had to appear in front of what was to all intents and purposes a hostile audience at the outset.

For quite some time, January and February 1964 had been marked in the diaries of many opera lovers as the months when two major new productions by the renowned Franco Zeffirelli were to grace the stage of the Royal Opera House Covent Garden. In January Zeffirelli was to direct two legends in their own time, Maria Callas and Tito Gobbi, in a new staging of *Tosca*, followed almost immediately by a new staging of *Rigoletto* with Geraint Evans, one of the House's most popular and outstanding artists, in the title role. In the *Rigoletto* production, Anna Moffo and Carlo Cossutta, both highly regarded internationally, were to sing Gilda and the Duke of Mantua and the conductor was to be Georg Solti, now firmly established as the Royal Opera House's very successful, if controversial, Music Director. These occasions were undoubtedly two of the most eagerly anticipated events of the thriving Covent Garden Opera Company and expectations ran very high.

As it turned out, however, the new *Rigoletto* production seemed jinxed before it had made its entrance. In the early stages of rehearsal Geraint Evans began to encounter severe vocal difficulties and after a considerable amount of trouble the first night was cancelled. In the meantime Anna Moffo felt unwell and when the postponed first night, originally scheduled as the second performance, eventually arrived she was suffering from a fever whilst Geraint was struggling under great strain. A most unhappy evening, although it was memorable for something very special at the end. At his curtain call, Geraint waved his hand to ask the audience to stop applauding. He then asked them to forgive him for having sung a role he should not have taken on. They gave him the most tremendous ovation, and to this day my eyes well up with tears when I remember this wonderful gesture of honesty from Geraint and the emotional response from his audience, who loved him as one of their great favourites, as he deserved to be.

It had fallen to me to be the understudy who would cover Geraint in the title role. Although I was a very experienced

Rigoletto, I had never sung it in Italian and this had meant starting off again at the beginning in many ways. I slaved at it with even greater intensity than I usually gave to my work because I knew from the outset that Geraint, a superb singer of course, was not vocally made for Rigoletto and I was prepared for a call to take over the part. Frankly, I was ready for this from the moment the rehearsals began, when I was only in attendance as the cover, and so when the inevitable happened, which was immediately after the unfortunate postponed first night, I felt a tremendous surge of confidence at the thrilling opportunity to sing Rigoletto at Covent Garden in their prestigious new production by Franco Zeffirelli.

I now had just one day in which to rehearse the music and receive only a smattering of guidance about the staging for the next performance. There was no opportunity at all to go on to the stage to rehearse the production. When I sang the piano rehearsal for Solti, I put in the two traditional high A flats (at the word 'vendetta' in the scene where Rigoletto swears vengeance on the Duke of Mantua and at the very end of the opera when he lets out his terrible cry of despair after Gilda has died) as well as the high G in 'Pari siamo'. Immediately Solti told me these high notes were optional and he would not allow me to sing them as they had been taken out for Geraint's sake and he could not alter that decision. I protested that I had always sung them in the past instead of the lower notes that many baritones opt for because I could manage them and they were Verdi's original intention. Solti simply reinforced his position by saying that he had just recorded the opera with Robert Merrill, who, like Geraint, did not have the high notes in his register and he had promised Geraint that as far as the role of Rigoletto was concerned he would conduct at Covent Garden in the way that he had done on the recording, that is taking out those high notes. His dismissive attitude upset me and we had a heated discussion, at the end of which Solti said: 'We shall break now for lunch. Please ring your wife and explain the position to her so that she can maybe guide you, because if you continue in your intention to sing the high notes, then I can see no future for you at Covent Garden.' I took his advice and Joyce said 'Who cares about a few top notes at such an important period of your career? Everybody has heard you sing them, so you don't have to prove yourself.' I reluctantly agreed with her and started the afternoon rehearsal by informing Solti that I would go along with his decision.

I should say that my reluctance was nothing to do with ego. Verdi had originally wanted the high notes so as to make an extra special impact at those very intense moments. He wrote them as being optional because he was worried that the baritones of the time might not manage them within their range, but then the lower note options became the standard notes in the printed score. The famous coach and repetiteur Luigi Ricci, who was born whilst Verdi still was alive, bore this out when I was in Rome, later, singing Donizetti's *Roberto Devereux*. He produced the original parts of *Rigoletto* and there were the high A flats and the high G!

On Monday 10 February I arrived at the stage door of the Royal Opera House to sing my first Covent Garden performance of *Rigoletto*. This was to be the first time I was singing it in Italian, there had been only a modicum of rehearsal and as it was the originally scheduled third performance the BBC were to relay it on the radio. The audience had come to see Geraint, and they and the radio listeners were to find out that he was indisposed. Added to that, just before curtain up they were told by a nervous House Manager that Anna Moffo was suffering from a heavy cold and craved their indulgence. The evening began with boos, hisses and cat-calls, and Georg Solti had to wait for them to subside before making his entrance into the pit to begin the Prelude. As I walked down the stairs from my dressing room to the stage to get in place for my first appearance, for a few moments I had mixed feelings.

All apprehension immediately vanished the moment I went on. Although I was far too involved with the performance to be consciously thinking of anything else, deep down I knew this was the moment I had waited for ever since I had first been fired to be an opera singer when I had seen *Rigoletto* and *I Pagliacci* in Sheffield twenty-three years earlier. Even then, I could not have known what the outcome of this night would be. The proceedings were accurately reported the next day by Kenneth Loveland in *The South Wales Argus*. He wrote ' . . . However, an opera audience, having staged its initial protest at a change of cast and an announcement that Anna Moffo craved their indulgence for her having a cold, is always quick to forgive and forget and, in any event, Miss Moffo received at the end of the evening a substantial ovation which obviously moved her. This ovation was quite dwarfed by that given to Mr Glossop, and rightly so. Miss Moffo, I feel, even at the top of her form, would be quite miscast as Gilda. Mr Glossop, on the other hand has the makings of an outstanding Rigoletto.' Noel Goodwin in *The Daily Express* also reported that 'Mr Glossop, who was once a bank clerk, had been understudy since the new production by Franco Zeffirelli went into rehearsal . . . Last night he had to face an audience made hostile by the news that American soprano Anna Moffo had a cold. Shouts of "understudy" greeted the pre-curtain announcement that she had "courageously decided to appear". But in the end of the second scene the audience warmed to the performers, and at the third interval Mr Glossop won a tremendous ovation.'

There was one review that unintentionally had an ironic significance for me. Charles Reid, writing in *Punch*, concluded by saying 'Georg Solti conducts with unbridled verve an edition which restores passages that are usually cut and docks decorations and variations introduced by singers and conductors over the years. He also keeps his singers on a tight rein, never giving them as much head as tradition dictates at the summit of this phrase or that. It is all very prim and aseptic.' Despite Sir Georg Solti's fame in opera I have always maintained that he was never a singer's conductor. He only studied the scores rather than the way the music comes from the words. I used to say that for him, if the orchestra was not playing, even though two great singers were sustaining their top notes and thrilling the audience, nothing was happening. Of course his achievement at Covent Garden was impressive, but I was not alone in finding him dictatorial and even restrictive when it came to a singer's interpretation. He seemed to be suspicious of the artists' motives if they wanted some freedom. More often than not I feel he failed to understand that the finest singers are extremely disciplined in their approach to their music and are very concerned to be faithful to the composer's intentions. I know that some world famous singers enjoyed performing with Solti, but I found the experience unrewarding each time.

On 12 February I sang my second performance. During the second scene of the first act, whilst I was singing the duet with Anna Moffo, I turned for a moment to address Gilda's maid, Giovanna, and then as I turned my head back to Anna I just managed to grab her as she was falling to the floor. She had fainted. I continued singing and at the same time tried to gesticulate to Solti to bring the curtain down. This was to no avail and I finished the duet as a solo before the curtain came down at last. Anna was taken to her dressing room to recover and her understudy, Elizabeth Vaughan, was urgently sent for. Luckily she was at home washing her hair. She rushed to the theatre and in what seemed like a very short time I was singing the duet for the second time. Anna later blamed her faint on the pills she was taking for her fever. The *Daily Mirror*'s account of the event was taken from fairyland. Firstly, the headline was 'Covent Garden star faints in tenor's arms'. Then came 'Anna Moffo collapsed whilst singing the leading role in Verdi's *Rigoletto* at Covent Garden.' Whether they thought she was singing Rigoletto or whether they thought Gilda was the title role I will never know. I never bothered to tell them that she fainted in my arms whilst the tenor was having a rest in his dressing room.

Altogether I sang four performances of *Rigoletto*. The last one, on 19 February, was conducted by Edward Downes and I found him far more sympathetic than Solti, whilst still being very much in control – he had an ideal combination of precision and flexibility. He also assured me that in the forthcoming season, in which he was to conduct all the *Rigoletto* performances, all the high notes were to be restored! The world now knows that Ted Downes is not only one of the finest Verdi conductors but also one of the most erudite authorities on the performance of his music. I was one of many singers who learned gems of wisdom from him decades ago and the occasion of my Rigoletto was a case in point.

It just so happened that while the preliminary rehearsals for the new production at Covent Garden were in an early stage of progress, I was singing Rigoletto at Sadlers Wells, and as I was understudying Geraint at the Garden, Ted came to see my performance at the Wells. Actually, I think he was concerned that Geraint was not going to make the first night and so he wanted to check me out. He came up to me the day after one performance and told me he liked my interpretation very much but there were some places where it could be better. There was one particularly discerning point he made which was of the greatest value for me. In the second act, Rigoletto is cruelly thrown on to the floor by the courtiers as he desperately tries to open a door where he thinks Gilda is being kept. Ted said to me 'When you got up, you were far too fast coming up and starting to sing. Stay down. Then slowly put your head up. Then you begin singing.' I never forgot that – it made that moment ten times more dramatic and tragic.

When I later performed *Rigoletto* in a televised production from Parma, as always from the time of my Covent Garden début in the role I performed the scene where Rigoletto is thrown on to the ground exactly as Ted Downes had suggested. Not long afterwards, during a stay in Rome, my old friend and colleague the great baritone Tito Gobbi invited Joyce and me to dinner at his villa outside the city. There were about eight of us present, and at the end of the meal Tito said he wished to tell us a little story. He recounted how he had switched on the television to find a performance of *Rigoletto* in progress. He was particularly interested to see the famous 'Cortigiani' aria in the second act, which he had sung hundreds of times. He told us how impressed he was with the baritone singing Rigoletto and how he particularly admired the change in his character after being thrown on to the ground by the courtiers. It was so striking how after all his raging anger he stayed motionless on the floor and then only slowly got up before beginning to plead with them in tears for the return of his daughter. He said to us 'I said to myself "I wish I could do that!" ' Then he told us the name of the baritone was Peter Glossop. I was quite overcome that the great Gobbi could praise a fellow baritone in such a generous manner.

That moment of dramatic insight in *Rigoletto,* which had so impressed Gobbi, was the kind of gold that singers got from Ted Downes. I must also mention, in passing, the influence of Gobbi. I have always made a point of studying the performances of my baritone colleagues in order to garnish new ideas and improve my interpretations. I never alter my own identification of a role to copy anyone, rather I examine others' performances to add to and make better my own impersonation. Gobbi was a particularly special study for me, as he was for so many baritones of my generation.

The *Rigoletto* performances were a watershed for my international reputation, and undoubtedly this year of 1964 at the Royal Opera House opened the gateway to the world for me. I say this not as a boast but as a tribute to the way the House worked. I was a company member and so I was expected to fulfil daily duties in a wide variety of parts – only two nights after the last *Rigoletto* I was back on stage as Amonasro in a revival of *Aida*, with Galina Vishnevskaya as Aida, Jon Vickers as Radames and Giulietta Simionato as Amneris. The point is that Sir David Webster and his team saw to it that a company member could develop an international career while continuing to make Covent Garden the priority, provided the artist's real commitment to the Royal Opera House continued. The key to this was the strategy of giving company members major lead roles alongside famous international guest artists. That all disappeared later as the House began to lose its ensemble company whilst its managerial bureaucracy expanded. To be fair, it became much harder to keep artists with international reputations on contract as they increasingly wanted to enjoy the benefits of jet travel and spend much more time singing around the world as big stars. If he were alive today, Sir David Webster just would not be able to run the kind of ship he captained in his time. Even so, what he did achieve for his company of artists back then can never be over-estimated. Covent Garden gave singers like me the finest imaginable opportunities.

It was above all the music of my great hero Giuseppe Verdi that put me in the international limelight. As well as the *Rigoletto* performances both at Covent Garden and Sadlers Wells, I had by now sung my first Iago in *Otello*, with Scottish Opera, and later in the year I was to perform the role at Covent Garden, where I was also looking forward to singing di Luna in the important new *Il trovatore* production by Luchino Visconti that was to be conducted by Carlo Maria Giulini. All these performances, as well as my Rodrigo in *Don Carlos* at Covent Garden, were crucially to spread my name to the top Italian opera houses, but in the meantime my début in that glorious country had already been prepared for me by my new Italian agent Gabriele d'Averio. After the audition for the Italian Radio and Television Company (RAI), which he had arranged when I had been singing for Giulini in Rome the previous November, he had set up my first concert in Italy.

I was to sing in the RAI Martini Rossi Concerts, an immensely popular series that was broadcast all over Europe. The date was 11 June 1964 and I was given permission by Covent Garden to take part solely on condition that I would be in Manchester the next morning to rehearse *Otello* with Jon Vickers for both his and my début in the opera with the company. The only way I could make that work was to book my return flight to London on an eleven o'clock flight immediately after the concert and then drive straight from Heathrow Airport to Manchester to be in time for the rehearsal. I decided to go ahead, despite the risks and obstacles. I am glad I did so, because the concert was a huge success, and it directly led to

Di Luna in Il trovatore, *with Dame Gwyneth Jones*
as Leonore, Royal Opera House, 1964
(Donald Southern Collection at the Royal Opera House Archives,
by kind permission of the Royal Opera House)

a thrilling opportunity. At the concert was Dr Giuseppe Negri, the Intendant of the Parma Opera House, the theatre of the province where Verdi was born, and two days later he engaged me to sing three performances of *Rigoletto* the following season. That was really to be the start of the most rewarding time of my life, singing Verdi on his own soil, first at Parma and then at La Scala Opera House in Milan.

After the concert I had to rush into a taxi to be in time for the eleven o'clock flight to London. Fortunately there were no delays and I arrived at Heathrow at around midnight local time. I managed to get about four hours sleep and then started off in my car for Manchester which was a good six-hour drive in those pre-motorway days. When I arrived I was hoping I would be able to keep up my strength for the first rehearsal of *Otello*, only to be told that Jon Vickers was tired after his flight from Canada and had cancelled the rehearsal! Just imagine if I had decided not to take the risk of singing at the concert. There is no doubt it propelled me into the very top echelon of Italian opera.

It was a wonderful experience to sing with Jon in *Otello* and we were to perform together in this masterpiece for many years in different places, including the Salzburg Festival. Out of that arose Herbert von Karajan's film of the opera with Jon, Mirella Freni as Desdemona, and me. Meanwhile, for another several months it was still business as usual at Covent Garden as after the summer tour of the provinces ended I began my third season as a company member. In the first dozen or so weeks my main assignments were as varied and demanding as always: Iago in a revival of *Otello*, this time with James McCracken in the title role; Donner, a small part in Wagner's *Das Rheingold*; advance rehearsals for Britten's *Billy Budd*, singing the title role in an opera I had never seen and knew little about; and di Luna in the important new production of *Il trovatore*.

With the stage direction of Luchino Visconti, the casting of Bruno Prevedi, Leontyne Pryce and Giulietta Simionato and the conducting of Carlo Maria Giulini, *Il trovatore* promised to be another of Sir David Webster's prestigious new gala promotions, and it was yet another wonderful and, as it turned out, far-reaching opportunity for me in the music of the great Giuseppe Verdi. Although I had sung di Luna many times, to work on it with these great artists in such an important production brought me the strongest exposure since my Covent Garden *Rigoletto* – and my debut in Parma was only weeks away. Yet again, the rewards of being a member of Sir David Webster's Covent Garden Opera Company, soon to become the Royal Opera, were immense, all the time strengthening my international future.

Less than two weeks before the opening night, Leontyne Pryce cancelled. In her stead I found myself on stage with a young Welsh soprano called Gwyneth Jones, who had studied in Geneva as a mezzo-soprano and had changed only one year earlier to singing soprano. She was a simply wonderful Leonore and it was no surprise to me that she subsequently had a glorious career. From her mezzo-soprano days she had a rich and strong middle voice that now supported beautiful, soaring top notes. Coming in at short notice, she was greatly helped both by Visconti and Giulini – and directors and producers do not always help replacements, as I have intimated earlier in this memoir.

On the whole Visconti took a more traditional approach than Zeffirelli had done with his *Rigoletto*, although compared to what has been going on in opera during the last quarter of a century Zeffirelli was very traditional! On that point, I feel that a real artist interprets the genius of the creator and does not try to make himself or herself the genius. I go as far as to say that up to 90 per cent of all operas should in general be staged along the lines that they were first meant to be performed. For me, there has been so much tampering in recent years that opera is more often than not no longer the work that its composer conceived. So many of these new concept productions are to me just full of cheap tricks. By giving world famous opera directors so much power, the opera companies have now put many performers into straitjackets where they have to comply with a totally new view that can be very alien to them. Some artists enjoy these novelties – I find they are usually destructive to the composer and librettist.

The great joy for me in the new *Il trovatore* was Giulini. He is a true aristocrat, in the very finest sense of the word, and he is deeply intelligent. He was absolutely meticulous about details and style, but he was also kind. He persuaded and helped you to take his requests. 'You know this phrase – could you put more line in it, so that you match the phrase of the cello?' he would say. In addition to his special artistry he had technical mastery and had a wonderful way of communicating his wishes to the singers, the chorus and the orchestra, who all felt absolutely secure with him. I found him absolutely perfect as a conductor. He always looked at me whenever I was singing and there was total rapport. When you are singing an opera on stage, of course you have to have your eye on the conductor, but your pre-occupation is, naturally, with the words, music and action that you are performing. Giulini's great gift as an opera conductor was that he could allow you to perform but you were absolutely in no doubt as to where he was going.

During the interval of one of the piano rehearsals for *Il trovatore*, Giulini joined me for some tea in the staff canteen. 'You are looking a bit serious today,' he said to me. 'Well,' I explained, 'I am feeling apprehensive because after these performances I am going to Parma to make my debut singing *Rigoletto*. I have been told that not many singers want to sing at the Parma Opera House because they boo you off the stage if you make a single mistake in the language or if you crack a single note. Don't they call it "The Lion's Den"?' 'Yes they do,' replied Giulini, 'but they are not the worst audience, they are the best. They are such passionate advocates of Verdi, as he was born in Parma, that if you sing well you will have the greatest ovation you have ever known. It's only the bad singers who are in danger.' 'Maestro, you are being wonderfully helpful,' I said, 'but I still can't forget how Tito Gobbi told me that he has never sung in Parma because he feels it isn't worth the risk!' 'As Gobbi is booked all over the world,' he assured me, 'there is no reason for him to sing there, so why take the risk? But you have a wonderful voice, so just enjoy yourself and sing.' That was like a lifeline from Giulini for what was coming up as perhaps the most important event of my career.

CHAPTER FIVE

A Son of Italy

Parma is the birthplace of Verdi, and the public there regard themselves as the arbiters of how his works should be sung. On 22 December 1964 I arrived in the city, with the fortifying words of Giulini still ringing soothingly in my ears. What a thrill this was! For a boy from Sheffield to be making his début in one of the most famous opera houses in Italy, and singing the opera I loved more than any other – *Rigoletto*. And yet, at such a unique moment as this, the singer's greatest dread was descending. I was going down with a cold and I was to start rehearsals the very next day. There was no point trying to hide from the problem so I decided to 'mark' the rehearsals and sing in an undertone until the performances so as not to roughen my voice. I was going to let nothing destroy my very first opera performance in Italy. In the event, a bizarre incident before the first night helped to deflect the worry a little in a roundabout way.

The first opera of the new season in Parma was *Un ballo in maschera*. It took place on 26 December at half-past nine in the evening – the traditional date and time for the Teatro Regio's opening night. All the singers engaged to appear at the opera house, including me, were booked into the Hotel Jolly, just one block away from the theatre. At about midnight on the 26th I was awakened by a commotion in the corridor

Receiving an honorary degree from Sheffield University with, left to right, A. R. Clapham, W. H. Auden and Sir Kenneth Clark, 18 July 1970

outside my room. I realized that *Ballo* would still be running at the theatre, so this couldn't be the singers returning after the performance. The next morning I enquired what the noise was all about and I learned that at the beginning of the last act, Cornel McNeil, who was singing Renato, had thrown a tantrum at the beginning of the aria 'Eri tu' and had walked off the stage. He then locked himself in his dressing room and reappeared twenty minutes later in his outdoor clothes. Giuseppe Negri, the Intendant, tried to remonstrate with him but McNeil threw a punch at him and stormed out of the theatre. When he arrived back at the hotel, pursued by members of the opera house management, there was a violent confrontation outside his room and he had to be restrained. Meanwhile, the rest of that performance had been aborted. Not surprisingly, McNeil went back home to America, and another baritone sang the remaining two performances. I later learned that McNeil had to pay a substantial fine for his misdemeanour.

The major newspapers in Italy reported the furore at the Teatro Regio under the title 'Giallo a Parma!' I don't think McNeil sang in Italy again. All this a few days before my stage début in Italy, I was suffering from a cold, and the audience in the Lion's Den would now be more ready for the kill than ever. But I was to be in luck. One of the two basses singing Sam and Tom, the conspirators in *Ballo*, became a good friend and when I confided to him that I had a cold and was worried about my voice not being in good shape for my *Rigoletto* performances, he said 'Don't worry' and immediately went to his room to bring me a box of medicines. He chose the ones for me to use, told me how to take them and for the next few nights doctored me like a mother! I found out later that all Italian singers travel with boxes of medicine, so they cannot be taken by surprise, also that drugs forbidden in England can be bought freely in Italy. The medicines worked wonders. At the dress rehearsal I felt my strength coming back after the second act and at last I was able to let myself go for the great final act. This was the first time the Teatro Regio had really heard me sing, and after my last A flat, as the curtain came down, the whole company came on stage and cheered me. Personally, I am sure it was more a gesture of relief than a tribute, because if I had gone the same way as McNeil, where would their season have been? Maybe that crazy incident was an indirect booster for me in disguise?

The next night, 3 January 1965, was my opening. Gilda was sung by Margherita Rinaldi and the Duke of Mantua was Gianni Jaia. The conductor was Luciano Rosada. After the fiasco of *Ballo* a few nights earlier, the atmosphere from the opening bars of the prelude was electric with tension – and apprehension! But I knew immediately I began that this performance was going to be a tremendous success. I felt in top form and I remembered how Maestro Giulini had told me that if all was well this was the best audience in Italy. At the end they gave me an ovation that felt like the greatest I had ever received by far. The next day the newspapers even included how the *passionati* were waiting for me outside the stage door and carried me shoulder high back to my hotel a hundred yards away. It was the most wonderful feeling of my career, and to this day I remember that night as the most exciting of my life. I immediately felt that I was a 'son' of Italy, so to speak, and a real child of my beloved Giuseppe Verdi, in his own homeland.

And yet, this was only the beginning. News about opera travels very fast in Italy, and because of the success of our performances, RAI made a quick decision to televise the last night. This came as a complete surprise to all the company, especially as the lighting was the responsibility of the television producer. It was more like a concert performance in costume. However, all went well, and that television performance was none other than the one seen by Tito Gobbi, as I described in the last chapter. The day afterwards I was taken to the Parma Town Hall and in a small ceremony the officials watched Dr Negri award me the Verdi Gold Medal of Parma, which is only given to outstanding interpreters of major Verdi roles. I was very moved by this superb gift, especially as it was awarded for my début performances in Italy. And now came the greatest surprise of all, just a few days later when I was back home rehearsing for my opening performance of the Covent Garden Opera revival of *Rigoletto*. Unknown to me, due to the exceptional press I had received, the management of La Scala Opera House in Milan had sent someone down to Parma to see the second night of *Rigoletto*. I was at home when the phone rang and immediately I recognized the voice of my agent Sandor

Gorlinsky. 'Peter,' he said 'you have cracked the biggest test of all. Francesco Siciliani, the Intendant of La Scala, has booked you and Margherita Rinaldi to open the next season in *Rigoletto*.' And the tenor was to be my very good friend Luciano Pavarotti, who would also be making his début at La Scala. So, I finally learned how to walk on air.

* * *

I will forever be indebted to Gabriele D'Averio for looking after my Italian introductions so astutely. The Martini Rossi concert in June 1964 had led to the Parma engagement and another important début for me, this time in Palermo, where I sang five performances of Père Germont in *La traviata* beginning on 18 February 1965. Now the exalted La Scala was on the horizon, entirely as a result of the Parma performances, and altogether in a very short space of time I was building a thriving new career in the country that was to become my very favourite land. Even so, one must never be too confident. In June 1965 I drove to Spoleto to sing Iago in a new production of *Otello* at the Festival of Two Worlds, the name given to the (at that time) Spoleto Festival of Opera. This was the creation of the composer Gian-Carlo Menotti who had given the first performances of several of his operas at the small Tuscan theatre in Spoleto, within travelling distance of Rome. Menotti had contacted my agent, but when Gorlinsky quoted my fee, Menotti wrote to him that it was more than Spoleto could afford. He asked if I could be persuaded to perform for a smaller fee, saying that 'sometimes we must help the poor'. I agreed, as a Tuscan town in summer sounded attractive. The best way I can recount what happened when I arrived is to quote in full Sydney Edwards of the *Evening Standard* who was in Spoleto for the Festival.

'The British have been doing well at this Festival. Peter

Glossop of Covent Garden has had personal success at the Festival singing Iago in a production of Verdi's *Otello*. Glossop, 37, a former bank clerk, made his name in Italy in January this year when he conquered the dreaded "Lion's pit" at Parma in a performance of *Rigoletto*. Since then he can do no wrong here and *The Times* the other day rashly announced Mr Glossop as the most popular Briton in Italy after James Bond.

'Glossop is a blunt Yorkshireman with a down-to-earth manner. He's not at all pleased with the Spoleto Festival and says so. He is upset at the way he was treated at rehearsals by the young American conductor Thomas Schippers, who besides being artistic director of the Festival also conducted and produced *Otello*. It was his first attempt at opera production and his efforts have been generally mauled by the critics. Glossop says: "Because I gave an interview which was construed as critical of Schippers, he has hardly spoken to me and I've been snubbed. I wouldn't mind if I had not come here in the first place as a direct result of a plea by Menotti, because they were in a jam, and I came at a much reduced fee because Menotti sent a telegram saying 'you must help the poor'. Schippers addressed me at rehearsal in a way I've never been spoken to before. Finally I had to take him aside and speak to him. Then when his underling assistants started calling me Glossop I lost my temper. I told them the name was Signor Glossop and if they called me by my surname again I'd punch them in the head. It's Signor Glossop now!" ' I know I reacted intensely, but I was hurt and shocked by the entire incident. Fortunately the performances were acclaimed by both the British and Italian press, so there was no damage ahead of the big début coming up in December.

It was partly because of the forthcoming *Rigoletto* at La Scala and also because I was being offered so many engagements in

Europe and also now Canada and the United States that I decided the time had come to leave the Covent Garden Company after two and a half wonderful years. I am one of many artists who acknowledge the tremendous benefit of having been a member under Sir David Webster's magnificent leadership. Happily I was to return regularly as a guest to take part in many more performances and indeed later in that year of 1965 I was singing di Luna in a revival of *Il trovatore* with Carlo Bergonzi, Gwyneth Jones and Fiorenza Cossotto. On many of the same nights, incidentally, my wife was being hailed as one of the finest Carmens of the time at the Sadlers Wells Opera and in the meantime I had made my début with the Canadian Opera Company in Toronto singing *Rigoletto* and Marcello in *La Bohème*. It was a remarkable year for our family, and the climax was coming right now as I made my way back to Italy on 23 November.

Most opera singers regard performing at La Scala in Milan as the acme of their careers. This is especially the case with foreigners, as Italy has more opera artists and theatres than any other country, and the non-Italians face very stiff opposition. Also the Italian audiences savour every word and note of their own repertoire and demand that the foreigners who appear at La Scala sing with perfect Italian pronunciation. So, when the rehearsals for *Rigoletto* began, Gabriele D'Averio came up from Rome to give me support and I have never been more grateful to anyone than I was for his help and advice at a time like that. Gabriele was more of a brother to me than an agent.

Also present at many of the rehearsals was Francesco Siciliani, the Intendant of La Scala, and Gabriele explained to me why. The previous two revivals of *Rigoletto* at La Scala had both failed. The first had featured Leonard Warren from the New York Metropolitan Opera, and for some reason the Milanese public had not taken to him. The next revival was with Ettore Bastianini, a favourite baritone of La Scala, but he had not sung well and was given a bad reception. Only later did the Milanese discover that he had developed throat cancer and indeed he was dead within a few years. After these two unfortunate *Rigoletto* revivals, Siciliani was particularly concerned that this third revival coming up now should go down well with the public. Not for the first time in my life was I about to make a crucial appearance in my career to a background of crisis in the theatre where I was going to perform.

At the dress rehearsal a man came to see me in my dressing room. He was the 'Capo del Claque' and Gabriele immediately came to terms with him. I was not happy at all about this Italian tradition of paying the claque, but Gabriele explained that if I didn't I could very well be booed and my performance could be ruined. He also explained that the management supported the claque because they would lead the audience with applause and bravos at all the right moments, which helped to make a good atmosphere for the opera! So, as they say, 'When in Rome do as the Romans do', and that definitely goes for Milan as well.

The opening night of *Rigoletto* at La Scala Opera House in Milan was on 9 December. This was the wish of a lifetime and I was absolutely ready for it. I felt very strong and determined about this most important moment in my career, even though it was daunting to have Signor Siciliani come up to me just before we began and, with the best of intentions, say 'Buona fortuna – coraggio!' Understandably, he was more nervous than any of us, but I am sure that must have disappeared very quickly because the performance went superbly from start to finish and the audience was already ecstatic at the end of the first act. At last Signor Siciliani had a success with *Rigoletto* at La Scala.

Making up before going on the stage of
La Scala Opera House as Rigoletto

The atmosphere really was fantastic that night. The superb lyric tenor of Luciano Pavarotti, making his début in the theatre like me, was made for the Duke of Mantua, in the way that I was for Rigoletto. Margherita Rinaldi was an outstanding lyric

Début at La Scala Opera House, Milan, 1965 – Rigoletto

soprano with a first-rate technique, and the conductor was a fine expert in Italian opera, Francesco Molinari-Pradelli (he was also an avid art lover – his house in Bologna was filled with beautiful paintings). With such a finely integrated group of musicians, the performance could not go wrong, and the public and press were marvellous to us. For my part, I received some of the most enthusiastic notices of my life and I feel it is only right to say now that although artists are frustrated when reviewers are inaccurate or uninformed, as they can be quite apart from their subjective opinions, there are surely few performers who do not appreciate recognition if it is appropriate. That has to be said with humility.

This is the time to pay my tribute to Italy and the Italian people. I was treated with such genuine generosity and courtesy and given such strong support by the managements and the audiences in virtually all the Italian opera houses in which I appeared that I felt I had become an Italian myself. The Italian people adopted me as one of their own and this was like a real and wonderful home, where the country as a whole loved and appreciated great opera with their hearts and souls. Ever since, I have never felt happier than when I have been in Italy, whether or not I have been singing.

My Italian schedule was hectic. In between performances of *Rigoletto* at La Scala I sang for the first time the title role in Verdi's *Simon Boccanegra* in Parma. Then in the first week of 1966 I went to Reggio Emilia, Bologna and Modena where the Parma production toured. It was exactly a year since I had made my Italian stage début with the company in *Rigoletto*, and I was now more embedded in the Italian opera scene than I could ever have imagined in my wildest dreams of only a few years earlier. I sang for six memorable years at La Scala, until someone with whom I had crossed swords elsewhere became all-powerful at the theatre.

I happened to be in Rome with Luigi Ricci, the famous head coach of the Rome Opera, when I was invited to be the guest of honour at a performance of *Eugene Onegin*. The stage director had decided that ballet dancers would sometimes 'interpret' the action by coming on stage from behind a pillar and dancing when the singers were not performing. To me that is stupid and insulting to Tchaikovsky and it was only one of many of the director's ideas that I found distracting and totally out of keeping with the music and the action. After the performance, the Intendant of the Rome Opera, Massimo Bogianchino, asked me what I thought about the production and I told him what I felt. I knew he was put out, but there was no way I could pretend to him. Despite this, he soon afterwards asked Gabriele D'Averio if I would sing six performances of Donizetti's *Roberto Devereux* at Rome, which could be tied into four performances of *Aida* at the open-air Caracalla Theatre. I turned that down because I did not want to learn a long opera that I was sure I would never sing again (although actually I was to record it two years later, by a strange coincidence) and also because the Palermo Opera had offered me the role of Don Carlo in Verdi's *La forza del destino* and I had to learn that for the first time. That apparently angered Signor Bogianchino even more than my opinion of his *Eugene Onegin*. So the scene was firmly set for a showdown when, in 1972, he was appointed the Intendant of La Scala Opera House. He immediately cancelled my contract to sing Posa in *Don Carlos* the following season, but when I asked Sandor Gorlinsky to sue him he said that if we did so I would probably never sing again in Italy. Signor Bogianchino remained at La Scala for some time and so I never did sing again at that wonderful opera house. It was a sad ending to the most rewarding time of my career, but I did not regret what I had said and done and I do not to this day.

It was while I was singing at La Scala in *Un ballo in maschera* that I had my first encounter with Herbert von Karajan. The baritone engaged to sing Tonio in Leoncavallo's *I Pagliacci*, Giacomo Guelfi, had dropped out at short notice, saying that Alfio in Mascagni's *Cavalleria Rusticana* was enough for him to sing in one evening (however I had heard that his high A flat at the end of the Prologue in *I Pagliacci* was doubtful – and that is not a worry to have before singing at La Scala!). As *Cavalleria Rusticana* was to be followed, as is traditional, by *I Pagliacci*, I mentioned to Signor Siciliani that I had sung the work many times and could maybe help out, as they would now need to find a replacement for the baritone in that opera. He said immediately he would like me to do this, however Herbert von Karajan would be conducting the opera and he had total rights to the casting. I would have to audition for him.

It happened that I was going to London for two days to finalise the sale of my house, and this was a real blessing. It was the role of Tonio that I was to sing to Karajan, but I had only sung Silvio before, so I immediately called John Matheson, who was coaching at Covent Garden, and asked if he could crash course Tonio with me in Italian. As a result, two days later when Karajan heard me sing the Prologue he immediately accepted me for the performances. As it turned out, for reasons I will not go into now, after a week of rehearsal both operas were cancelled, but Karajan had already booked the ice-rink in Milan to make a film of both *Cavalleria Rusticana* and *I Pagliacci*, which he would be conducting and directing together with a screen producer. So this was in fact the first time I sang with the maestro who was the most famous and powerful conductor of his time. I will speak about him in more detail later on, but for now I will end this memoir of my induction into Italy with an explanation of how Herbert von Karajan's words have landed on the introductory resumé of this book. For the film of *I Pagliacci* we recorded the sound track first with the La Scala Orchestra and after that we mimed the words during the filming of the opera. It was at a playback when Karajan saw me as Tonio surreptitiously looking round corners that he said 'that's who I want for my Iago – I must have his eyes!' The result, of course was that he immediately booked me to sing Iago in his new production of *Otello* at the Salzburg Festival.

CHAPTER SIX

Some Thoughts on Verdi

Verdi opened up unprecedented vistas for the singer. As well as requiring a wider range of dramatic and lyrical expression than his predecessors in Italian opera, his works made vast new demands on the singer's acting ability – acting both theatrically and with the voice itself. In Verdi's operas it is crucial that the performer can sing most beautifully when needed but also have the capacity to express the words in a highly dramatic way.

In his baritone roles Verdi wrote music that combines the styles of the dramatic, heavy bass baritone and the light, comic buffo. In his time, this meant that there had to be a new type of baritone with a big voice but also great agility. There had to be overall strength, high range and resilience in the low register. The Verdi baritone certainly has to be able to handle a top G and if possible also an A flat and yet he also has to have a depth and richness to be a father like Germont, Rigoletto, Philip the Second, or the Miller (in *Luisa Miller*). Not many baritones have both the high range and the darkness of timbre as well as the brilliant agility. I was just lucky that I did have those qualities in my voice, and as I loved Verdi so deeply from the very first moment I ever saw one of his operas, I decided to labour intensively to develop my vocal and acting attributes so as to do justice to his roles as best I could. This chapter is a glance at some of his greatest baritone parts viewed from the perspective of my long experience singing them on stage.

When I first studied a Verdi role, I never began with the music. I always made a detailed study of the libretto first, so as to understand the story and characters as Verdi saw them before he began to set them to music. This was my procedure with all operatic parts, but for me it was especially important in Verdi. I started where Verdi started and formed my own thoughts on the story, just in the way that he worked. After this I studied the music and listened to it in my mind and, as I did so with the knowledge of the libretto, I began to understand why Verdi wrote what he did. I do not believe a singer can attempt to interpret a part properly unless he or she has approached the role in this way. Studying the music and the words together at the beginning deprives the singer of a true comprehension of what the composer has written.

Never is this more crucial than in the operas of Verdi, who was so particularly immersed in the words' expression before he set them to music. For instance, sometimes I was surprised at the way he had reacted to a particular word or set of words, and this vitally affected my way of interpreting what he had written. Verdi's innovation was that he went far further than writing just beautiful tunes to the words he had read. He was composing new inflections and colours for the voice's expression of the words, and these will be lost in the interpretation if the singer cannot hear them in direct relation to the words, i.e. outside the melody. Verdi was such a wonderfully melodic composer that it is all too easy to become lost in his melodies. Singers can sound wonderful if they master those melodies alone, but to interpret the characters that Verdi evoked you have to know what it is the melody is expressing and then colour it. There are times when you can translate the same Verdi melody either in a sweet, sugary way or in a strong, robust way, but if you look at the words they will tell you whether it should be sweet, strong, half-voiced etc.

*   *   *

Macbeth was Verdi's most daringly innovative work to date when it appeared in 1847. It called for a whole new range of vocal and theatrical expression in opera, and the title role of *Macbeth* was an unheard-of challenge for a singer who had to go far further than merely singing melodically or dramatically. Verdi specifically stipulated many new psychological and theatrical elements in the voice and he extended these even more when he came to revise the opera in 1865.

I have sung both the original 1847 version and the revised 1865 version, which is far more often performed. Among a number of important changes in the revised version is a duet between Macbeth and Lady Macbeth at the end of the third act. It replaces a big solo aria for Macbeth in the 1847 version, and I can see why Verdi did this. That aria really is quite bombastic, which I do not mean in a derogatory sense at all as it is wonderfully impressive, but it is in a style noticeably different from the subtle duet that replaced it in the revision. When you perform the revised opera you do feel that Verdi had said to himself that the aria was cruder. Nonetheless, although I maintain that one must respect Verdi's judgement in revising his work, it is very important that we should be able to hear the remarkable novelty and adventurousness of his *Macbeth* as he originally wrote it. The later *Macbeth* may be more sophisticated, but in any case some of the most arrestingly dramatic music of all was retained from the original in the revision, and even the extraordinary Sleepwalking scene is, on the whole, similar in both. From the beginning of its existence, this opera opened up a striking new world of vocal and theatrical expression for the singer.

There are people who have cavilled that musical settings of Shakespeare detract from the truth and power of the Bard's creations. For me, in *Macbeth, Otello* and *Falstaff*, Verdi was able to enhance Shakespeare's plays with expressive colours that are absolutely in keeping with the characters and sentiments of the originals, even if he and his librettists had to make changes and cuts for practical purposes. I think it is highly significant that when Verdi was rehearsing the baritone Felice Varesi for the premiere of *Macbeth*, he told him he should pay more attention to the words than the music, to serve the poet more than the composer. That was a revolutionary concept in opera and it shows how Verdi was striving to express the absolute truth of Shakespeare's creation. It also gives us the basis of how singers must approach their studies of his operas – through the words in the first instance. Verdi expected this of singers and that is notably implied when he said that the big duet between Macbeth and Lady Macbeth and the Sleepwalking scene 'must definitely not be sung. They must be acted and declaimed in a voice hollow and veiled – otherwise the effect will be lost.'

The role of Macbeth calls for a new scale of dynamic and expressive extremes in the operatic repertoire. Verdi was evoking the full intensity of Macbeth's reactions, and to understand them and his treatment of them properly we have to take into account the era in which the play was written. It was an age in which people absolutely believed in apparitions, spirits and ghosts. For Shakespeare these elements were real and true. If we look at them in terms of today's psychological thinking, we say that they were in the imagination. However Verdi wrote music that reflected Shakespeare's feelings and beliefs: he and his audiences believed that a ghost did come in and sit at a table as it does in *Macbeth*. It is vital to understand this state of mind when performing *Macbeth*, otherwise you cannot really interpret the extremes of his musical outbursts in the right way, with the sound of real fear. I feel particularly strongly about this in the case of this opera when it comes to stage production. If you set it in an age where there is no belief in these elements you just cannot make sense of the music that Verdi wrote.

*   *   *

Verdi's next major stylistic advance was his adaptation of the cruel story that Victor Hugo related in his play *Le Roi s'amuse*. *Rigoletto* exploded on to the stage of the La Fenice theatre in Venice on 11 March 1851 and the audience was spellbound. They had never seen or heard an opera remotely like it before. This was intense, confrontational music-theatre that grabbed them by the throat from the first, sinister notes of the Prelude. As for the title role, they had never experienced an operatic study of a torn character like this before.

The entire interpretation of *Rigoletto* as an opera, by the director, the conductor and the baritone in the title role, requires a very delicate balance between the extremes of tenderness and violence that personify the title role's contradictory poles of personality. Rigoletto himself is three people. First, over and above everything else, he is a loving and adoring father. Second, he is a professional jester whose job is to amuse the Duke of Mantua – his livelihood entirely depends on his skill at making fun of people. But third, he is full of vitriolic hate for the court, the people he mocks, as they detest him. Verdi writes music of great extremes for him. The voice needs to alter between sounding lyrical, tormented and violent. Rigoletto has to be a strong dramatic baritone but he also has to sing with pure *bel canto* in his most expressive moments.

I do not feel that Rigoletto's love for his daughter Gilda is unhealthy in any way at all. His possessiveness is born out of his fear for her and he has reason to be afraid for her safety in the appallingly immoral environment of the court of Mantua. When he is with her, he is basically his real self – tender and genuinely loving. The way he behaves most of the rest of the time is forced upon him by his dreadful circumstances. He is constantly suffering and he has no way out. He is pitifully deformed, he has lost his wife, who loved him despite his looks, and he has to bring his beloved daughter up so that she can survive. The only way he can earn his living to provide for both of them is by mocking people provocatively to excite the Duke of Mantua's sadistic sense of fun. He hates his job, and yet the complexity of his situation is such that it actually provides a release for him as he can openly express his violent hatred of the courtiers under the apparently legitimate guise of his profession. Or so it seems, until he goes too far and is cursed by Monterone.

But Rigoletto is more than just a tragic victim. He is courageous and not in the least bit afraid for himself, even though he is devastated by the curse. Yes, he hires Sparafucile to kill the Duke – yes that is a terrible thing to do, on the face of it. But just consider the circumstances. The Duke raped his daughter and humiliated her in his sick and corrupt court. I have two daughters. As I write this, my youngest is nineteen, just three years older than Gilda in Verdi's opera. I ask myself what I would do now if my daughter were raped. I think I would kill the bastard – and because I could not get away with it I would get someone else to do it. Yes, I would.

The awful tragedy about Rigoletto is that on behalf of his

beloved daughter he actually tries with his meagre forces to match the far greater forces of the Duke. And I do not just mean material forces. It is the cruel forces of nature and fate that finally defeat him. The Duke may be a monster, but his fatal charm and good looks protect him all the way. When Gilda overhears Sparafucile saying to his sister Maddalena that, because she wants the Duke's life to be spared, should someone call at their inn before midnight he will agree to kill whoever it is instead of the Duke and put that person's body in the sack for Rigoletto to throw into the river, Gilda decides to save the Duke by calling at the inn. There is the terrible irony – both nature and chance make and save the Duke of Mantua, and both nature and chance mark and finally destroy Rigoletto, whose only remaining source of life, Gilda, is now taken from him. For me, it is because he has been brave, albeit with his flaws, that the final tragedy is so unbearably heartbreaking, and I tried to convey that when I performed the role.

The final minutes of the opera need the greatest control. Rigoletto is horrified when he discovers Gilda in the sack, but she is still just alive and, although he realises there is hardly any hope at all, he does not know for sure that she will die within minutes. She is bleeding profusely, but he tries to convince himself that she might recover. When he pleads to her 'Do not leave me, stay with me', he is trying to bring her strength back to fight for her life. Whilst there is life there is hope. Rigoletto has to be very strong at this moment, because he is terrified Gilda may die, but now more than ever before in his life he has to make her feel safe and protected. In his heart he does really know it is hopeless, but he won't give in. He shows great dignity in this scene. As he cajoles and comforts his daughter, he has to sing with great beauty, somehow almost managing to hide the terrible pain he is in, because at this most dreadful time he will do all he can for her. And so, when he fails, his final outcry is a scream of complete despair.

*   *   *

It was in 1879 that the poet and composer Arrigo Boito and the publisher Giulio Ricordi first attempted to interest Verdi in writing an opera on the subject of Shakespeare's *Othello*. Eight unpredictable years were to pass before their dream came true and Verdi completed what many feel is his greatest and most original work. It is the inspired result of the composer's profound love and reverence for Shakespeare, whom he had studied and absorbed in the greatest depth. Critics have complained that the opera truncates the play considerably, but for me Verdi has totally mastered Shakespeare's subject.

It was in fact the role of Iago that most fascinated Verdi and at one time he even considered calling the opera *Iago* rather than *Otello*. I was in a privileged position in that I sang Iago as an Englishman who had been able to study Shakespeare's character in the original language, my own language, and so obtain nuances that a foreign translation just cannot carry. It is the insinuation in Iago's language that is so central to his character and his actions. Iago is insinuating in ninety per cent of the words he speaks. Once you look for that in the words and then listen for it in Verdi's music you will find the musical colour of Iago, because despite Verdi's reliance on an Italian translation his genius enabled him to assimilate Shakespeare's character and capture it in his music. Notwithstanding Verdi's success, as usual it is essential to study the words very carefully first of all in order to understand the composer's writing fully. It is a particularly subtle matter with the role of Iago as it is the degree of insinuation in the performance that will make him either credible or unconvincing.

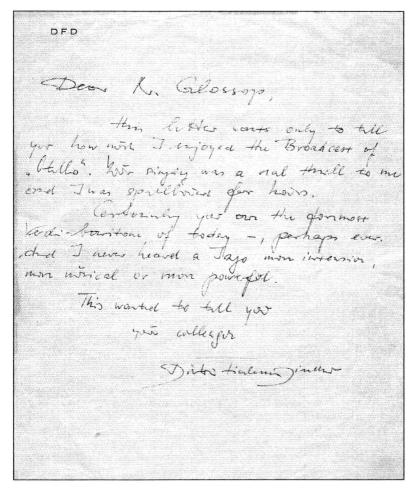

A prized letter from Dietrich Fischer-Dieskau
about my performance of Iago

You will only make Iago real if you grasp the pace at which he moves to bring Otello down. Although in the opera he moves quickly compared to the play, he must give the impression of hardly moving at all, as it is his oblique manner that undermines Otello so covertly. So much of the time he exerts his power through musical understatement. In the opera, the centre of his operation arrives at the end of the second act when he tells Otello his fabricated story about Cassio's dream of Desdemona. Verdi indicates that this short aria, 'Era la notte', must be sung as quietly as possible, and yet it is really the dramatic turning point, as it is now that Otello finally starts to succumb to Iago's deceit. It is so telling of Verdi to make this crucial moment almost a confidential but intimating whisper, and it is a great challenge to the singer to bring it off. Whenever I performed it I had in mind that at this very moment Iago makes his decision that he is going to put everything into the ring. This is going to be the greatest lie he has ever told. If he loses, he will die. He scores because he has chosen exactly the right moment to excite Otello to craziness. From now onwards Otello is in Iago's pocket.

The great secret of performing Iago is to sing in the most relaxed possible way. Just imagine – if he had tautness or sharpness in his tone, would you not sense something? He does what everybody would do in that situation. That is the terrible subtlety of the man. Iago dare not risk this mighty warrior, Otello, suspecting him. The only time you find out who Iago really is comes when he is on his own. His credo in the second act, which has often been criticized as an inappropriate interpolation on Shakespeare by Verdi and Boito, is there to identify Iago and study him on his own. Apart from this monologue and the moment at the very end of the third act when he kicks the unconscious Otello on the ground with 'Ecco il leone!' – 'look at the Lion [of Rome]!' – Iago has to sing in a deceptively restrained way. That is how he infects Otello, and that is his real frightening power, like an undetected virus.

Iago gloating over the unconscious Otello (Jon Vickers), Salzburg Festival, 1970 (Salzburg Festival Archive / Foto Madner)

Verdi very precisely marks how to do this in his score, and he and Boito are very faithful to Shakespeare's words here. If you follow Verdi's markings and sing Iago in an apparently straight-forward way you really will make him credible. That can be particularly hard when you have to sing very quietly and expressively in 'Era la notte', but there is no doubt at all about Verdi's intentions. His genius was to translate the true essence of Shakespeare's Iago into music and therefore the way the operatic part is acted must be in absolute accord with this.

As much as possible, I tried to avoid any suggestion of malice in Iago's facial expression, in keeping with the music's decep-tive understatements. For me this is an essential issue. If I may say so, I felt that Tito Gobbi, a magnificent Iago and a great artist whom I admired enormously, mistakenly allowed himself some evil-looking gestures when he performed the role. In real life Iago would never dare to do this, because someone might see him. Remember, Iago is Otello's trusted friend – 'Dear Sir, I am your servant. I can only give my life to you.' When Otello sees Iago he can only see a faithful servant in him, and that is how Iago is perceived by almost everyone else in the opera too. So, in the second act when Iago first begins to unsettle Otello, he must appear and also sound genuinely concerned for him, almost gently reassuring. Then, later in the act, in the one brief scene in the opera where Otello thinks he may have his doubts about Iago and violently throws him on to the ground, it is crucial that in the tone of his voice and the expression on his face Iago should appear wounded, not angry. He is saying 'I am your friend – would you think that I could do such a terrible thing as to deceive you? Sir, you insult me.' It is so important to be convincing at this moment, because Otello then says 'stay – maybe you are honest' and after wrangling with himself about whether Desdemona or Iago is being honest he demands that

Iago give him some proof. By remaining relatively calm and collected but appearing genuinely hurt, Iago has manipulated Otello into listening to him and he then begins his story about Cassio's dream. This episode needs the greatest care and control in Iago's voice and acting – the slightest excess will destroy the real power Iago exerts over Otello here.

To perform Iago really successfully the singer has to feel that he believes his lies when he tells them, that he is actually being truthful to himself at those moments. It will not work trying to be two people all at once. Iago is two separate persons at different times: when he is on his own he reveals his full real self but when he is with Otello, in his mind he is totally honest. This is all conveyed in Verdi's writing. Iago is a level-headed ensign and Otello is an excitable commander, and Iago's music often has the stability of conviction and assurance in contrast to Otello's music, which often has the instability of suspicion and consternation. At the same time, Iago can sing very suggestively in order to arouse Otello's feelings, as for instance in 'Era la notte', for which Verdi gives the singer meticulous indications of the vocal colour, nuance and character required. If you follow those markings really precisely this is a profoundly convincing fantasy both for Iago and Otello. Throughout the opera, Iago prepares everything subtly and gently, nearly always intimating to Otello that what he is suggesting should not necessarily be taken as certain truth – it is for Otello to decide and take the responsibility for that. But Iago will always faithfully stand by him, whatever.

*   *   *

The majority of Verdi's baritone roles portray men who are either middle-aged or elderly. For a young baritone that can seem very daunting, but Verdi gives you all the assistance you need in making the characters realistic if you precisely follow his markings. For instance, in *Simon Boccanegra* the wonderful duet with his daughter immediately establishes him as an older man and the powerful commander of Genoa. If when you are learning the work you keep that great aria in your mind from the beginning of the first Act you will feel you are a man of experience and gravitas. Similarly with Père Germont in *La traviata*, if you observe the lines and contours of Verdi's phrases and the dynamic instructions you will sound like a proud and patriarchal man of upper middle age. Verdi knew how to write different lines and colours for older and younger men. Even if you are a young baritone, you will capture the darker colours of the older, mature man if you accurately observe the shapes and dynamic shadings of Verdi's vocal lines. This is all by way of saying that the essence of singing Verdi is an absolute adherence to all the minute details of his vocal writing. Of course you have to act with imagination and intelligence too, and in all great music you have to observe the composer's markings meticulously, but no opera composer was more demanding, precise and indicative of a profusion of fine details in his scores than Giuseppe Verdi.

CHAPTER SEVEN

Benjamin Britten – A Memoir

From the moment I first sang in Britten's *A Midsummer Night's Dream* at Edinburgh in 1961 I loved the music of this remarkable genius, who I personally consider was the last great operatic composer. It was a wonderful thrill to have the privilege of singing with him on a number of occasions, culminating in recording the title role of Billy Budd under his direction in 1967.

When I was first approached by the English Opera Group in 1960 I must be honest and say that I did not think that this was going to my cup of tea at all. I had heard of the company, and knew that it had been founded and was directed by Benjamin Britten, but at that time I just was not interested. I was deeply involved with dramatic parts in the operatic repertoire of the nineteenth century and early twentieth century, and I felt I was aeons away in temperament from Britten's operatic world, which by then had become far removed in scale from the kind of environment I so loved. Nevertheless I accepted the engagement to sing Demetrius in *A Midsummer Night's Dream* as this was an opportunity to perform at the Edinburgh Festival. What a revelation it then was to discover the beauty and magic in this opera. I immediately realised that Britten had a wonderful theatrical gift and so when he came to see me one night in Edinburgh and asked if I would sing the role of

Tarquinius in his *The Rape of Lucretia* the following year I immediately accepted. This was the start of a very happy relationship between us and I have particularly cherished it ever since.

It was in 1963 that I received a telephone call out of the blue from Peter Pears inviting me to take part with him, Ben Britten and Galina Vishnevskaya in an operatic recital at the Aldeburgh Festival. I was thrilled and said yes, of course. Ben then came to the phone and told me he was going to include the Nile Duet from *Aida* as Galina and I were performing it at Covent Garden. He also wanted some extracts from operas of two of his favourite composers, Mozart and Tchaikovsky. The Tchaikovsky was to be *Eugene Onegin*, which I knew and loved, but had only sung in English. Galina was the reigning Tatyana at the Bolshoi and so for the recital we had to sing in Russian. Fortunately at Covent Garden, amongst the marvellous music staff of the time was a coach who specialised in the Russian language. I got together with him several weeks before the concert and prepared my solo aria in the first act and the final great duet between Onegin and Tatyana that closes the opera.

This was a fantastic event that I will never forget. Ben played the piano for the entire concert, with the Countess of Harewood his page-turner. He had a magic touch on the piano, which moved me very much. He was also such a wonderfully gifted and intelligent musician. Whether it was Mozart, Verdi or Tchaikovsky, he always had exactly the right tempo and feeling for the music. Added to that he was an inspirational artist to work with. Peter and I performed a duet from *Cosi fan tutte* and in one particular place Ben was extremely concerned that we should make the transition from the end of one phrase to the beginning of the next one not only with as clean as possible an attack on the new phrase but also, at the same time, with a feeling of ceaselessly continuing line from the last phrase, so that the change to the new key sounded magical. To make this effect work perfectly, he said, 'you do have to finish off the last phrase and start the new phrase cleanly, but so that we don't lose the line, if you take a very quick but hardly noticeable breath just before the new phrase it will come in with a feeling of surprise.' He so perfectly understood the essence and subtlety of Mozart's writing.

Two years later, in 1965, while I was still a member of the Covent Garden Opera Company, I was cast in the title role of *Billy Budd* for a revival of the opera, with Richard Lewis as Captain Vere and Forbes Robinson as Claggart, the villainous Master at Arms. The conductor was Meredith Davies. When I was selected, although it was a wonderful opportunity, I gave a lot of thought as to whether this really was a role I should sing.

Britten's setting of Herman Melville's novel about the traumatic conditions on board a British man-of-war at the end of the eighteenth century presents considerable difficulties for the artist playing the role of Billy Budd. Billy is a totally innocent person, a man who is so completely good that he cannot begin to imagine or understand anything about evil, and dies for it. The opera gives a harrowing portrayal of how he is victimised by his circumstances. I really had serious doubts whether I could take it on, both because it is so very hard indeed to play a character who is virtually without any faults at all, and also because I wondered if I really could seriously identify with the role. I talked the matter over with my wife Joyce and she said 'You can do it and you should go ahead with it.' So that is what I did.

Ben came to the first night of the revival of *Billy Budd*, on 26 April 1965, and beforehand sent me a telegram saying 'Best wishes for your first and wonderful Billy: Ben Britten'. It

Recording Billy Budd (photo by Hans Wild, by kind permission of Decca Records)

may have been as a result of these performances that I was subsequently engaged to take part in an ambitious full-scale television production of the opera that the BBC were to put on the following year with Peter Pears as Captain Vere, Michael Langdon as Claggart and Charles Mackerras conducting. Basil Coleman was to be the director.

The BBC's production of *Billy Budd* was something of a watershed in television opera and it turned out to be a vital event in my own career. I was delighted to be working again with Basil Coleman, who had produced Wagner's *The Flying Dutchman* for the Northern Opera when I had sung the title role with that company a few years before. He was a wonderfully sensitive and also highly imaginative director and he had a vital quality in an opera producer, which was a true knowledge and understanding of the relationships between the music, the words and the action. Not so many directors know and understand all three elements as they should! It was also marvellous to have Charles Mackerras as a masterly conductor and such a great support, especially as this was a very difficult undertaking. The opera is in itself extremely demanding, vocally and emotionally, and now there were additionally all kinds of technical complexities in the television production. Charles' profound knowledge of the score together with his command and experience of all the technical challenges thrown up in television productions were invaluable.

Ben Britten came to supervise the production from the time it was reaching an advanced stage of preparation. After we had finished all the filming I went to the BBC bar for a drink and in the middle of a thick crowd of people there was Ben with Peter. Immediately Ben saw me he fought his way through what must have been about thirty people to get to me. He put his arms round my neck and kissed me and said 'Peter – I've finally found my Billy Budd.' There and then he chose me for his recording of the opera, which he conducted for Decca the following year. The role of Billy Budd, which I had at first been so apprehensive about, was now one of my very 'own' parts.

Billy is a simple and honest young seaman who loves his life on the ocean and when his ship, a merchant vessel, is boarded by the Royal Navy press gang he is quite happy to be taken off by force to be placed on the danger-ridden warship the *Indomitable*. On the new ship he is unable to grasp the evil forces around him, principally embodied in Claggart, and he ultimately falls a tragic victim to fate. Claggart is so disturbed by Billy's simple goodness and his great popularity on the ship that his depravity overwhelms him and he manufactures a web of foul lies and intrigue against him, worthy of Iago. Finally, in front of Captain Vere, he hurls a string of vile, false accusations at Billy who is so stunned he cannot find a way of defending himself.

Billy's one serious flaw now overtakes him. When he is distressed he stammers and cannot speak properly and this time after groping around hopelessly for about half a minute, in his fury he instinctively strikes Claggart – killing him with the force of the blow. Now Vere has to make a terrible choice – he is sure Claggart was lying, and yet it is a time of war and the law decrees that Billy must be executed. Vere is certain Billy is innocent, but he has the responsibility of authority for the whole ship. He cannot allow what has happened to go by, and Billy himself recognises this. In his very last scene, Billy has a soliloquy, which Britten called 'Billy in the Darbies'. It is the only time in the opera that he sings solely to himself. He is in chains just a few hours, if that, before he goes to the gallows. Here, he realises that his Captain has no choice in his duty. He accepts Vere's decision and he does not hold it against him –

the Captain has his job to do, just like Billy has had his, as the ship's foretopman. So, Billy hangs.

Playing a man who is good is very much more difficult than taking on an evil character. How do you perform someone who is almost a Jesus Christ? If you are too bland you are idiotic. If you are too bold you are not giving the character the simplicity it calls for. I found it was much easier for people to cheer me when I was Iago or Rigoletto and far harder for them to respond so directly to me when I was Billy Budd, because Budd is an innocent. Now, how do you portray innocence? That is *very* difficult. I tried to play Billy Budd as a strong and forthright man and yet a simple and totally uncomplicated person. He is not stupid, and yet he is such a good person that he is fatally naïve – and I found that balance exceedingly demanding to bring off.

There has been opinion in some quarters of the operatic world that there are covert sexual innuendos in this work, that Captain Vere feels physical and emotional affection for Billy Budd, which subconsciously affects his final decision about his fate, and that John Claggart is repressing his physical feelings for Billy, which is why he sets out to destroy him. I cannot support this concept, which is uncorroborated in the text. My belief is that Vere simply admires a handsome and energetic sailor who is a credit to his crew. When Billy kills John Claggart, Vere knows full well he is innocent of deliberate murder, but under the Articles of War he feels he is powerless to alter the majority verdict of 'Guilty'. It is only in the Epilogue, as he looks back to the event in his old age, as indeed he does at the start of the opera, that Vere can say 'I could have saved him . . . O what have I done?' for his decision has tormented him ever since. As for Claggart repressing physical feelings for Billy, it is all too easy to imagine this if you decide to read such an association into Claggart's reference to his own depravity. But I believe Ben Britten was dealing with something far deeper and more fundamentally frightening than that. In setting Melville's text with such inspiration he was revealing the terrifying dark forces that are in man and which can destroy with such ferocious force.

When we came to make the Decca recording, I found Britten a delight to work with. He was meticulously precise and faultlessly clear, both in his intentions and his conducting, and he had absolute control of all the complex forces involved. Like Verdi, he always had a voice in mind for the parts he wrote, and yet I do believe that although he had written *Billy Budd* more than fifteen years before he came across me, he realised that I was the first Billy he had seen who could really make Captain Vere suffer with the terrible choice of decisions he has to make after Budd strikes Claggart dead. I do in all modesty believe that Ben Britten felt that I was the first Billy he had experienced who could set up the full tragedy of Vere. I believe that when he put his arms around me after the television recording and told me that he had finally discovered his real Billy Budd, this is what he had understood. Now, making this recording with him and a superb cast of singers, including Peter Pears as Vere and Michael Langdon as Claggart, was a wonderful climax to the association I was honoured to have with one of the truly great operatic composers.

CHAPTER EIGHT

Around the World in Twenty Years

When I left Covent Garden at the end of the summer of 1965, I was already receiving more international invitations than I could accept and during the next twenty years I managed to fulfil a scale of worldwide schedules that seems colossal when I look back on it now. I was regularly appearing in many theatres in Italy, Spain, France, Germany and Austria (especially the Vienna State Opera), I sang many times in the beautiful opera house in Buenos Aires, and I returned to the Royal Opera House as a guest every year until 1980, sometimes appearing in as many as four roles each season. Added to that, my début at the New York Metropolitan Opera led to a season singing there every year for fifteen years. In fact I was singing nearly all the time and sometimes I would be away from home for as much as six continuous months. For a start, each time I was engaged by the Metropolitan Opera I was there for two and a half months. That was because every year I was offered at least two roles and also asked to cover another two. It was the policy at the Met to have covers available all the time and the House paid half a fee for covering a role. So, effectively I was being paid for singing three roles when I would most likely only sing two, but if I did have to perform one of the roles I was covering I would then get a full fee for that part as well.

My début on the stage of the Metropolitan Opera was in

1971 when I sang the role of Scarpia in *Tosca*. Before that, though, I had made two appearances with the company in concert performances of operas at Newport, Rhode Island. I sang *Rigoletto* on 18 August 1967 and then the following week I replaced Tito Gobbi as Iago in a performance of *Otello* with the fabulous cast of Jon Vickers as Otello and Renata Tebaldi as Desdemona. After the *Otello* performance, I was invited by a friend of mine to a reception that was being given by Charlotte Ford, an heiress of the Ford family who was one of the most generous patrons of the arts. When I was introduced to her, the famous intendant of the Metropolitan Opera, Rudolph Bing, was with her. It was our very first meeting, but far from welcoming me, he was off-hand and patronising. It was obvious to me that he felt I should not be at the reception. I found that discourteous and unnecessary and I also couldn't help feeling that he was pulling rank over another Englishman whom he saw as an unknown new boy in the great empire he had built up in New York.

Although Bing was in fact Austrian (he had been born in Vienna), he had become the manager of the Glyndebourne Opera in 1936 and had built up his reputation as an admired opera administrator in England, where he took citizenship. After the war it was as a formidable Englishman that he went to New York to run the Metropolitan Opera, where his two decades were certainly regarded as a golden era by many. He was extremely proud of his achievement at the Met, and he had every right to be, but he came across to me as someone who wore his success haughtily. Nevertheless – he did re-engage me!

In May 1971 I arrived in New York to begin rehearsals at the Met for a run of performances of *Tosca*. Grace Bumbry was in the title role, Franco Corelli was Cavaradossi, and I was Scarpia.

At the very first rehearsal, a young conductor appeared whom the Metropolitan Opera had never seen before, but there was one person he did know and that was myself. I had already sung with the very gifted James Levine. He was to become the immensely successful Music Director, with one of the longest and most powerful reigns in operatic history. We had first met a few years earlier at Cardiff when my wife Joyce was singing Rosina in Rossini's *The Barber of Seville* with the Welsh National Opera. He had been the conductor of that production and shortly afterwards he was the conductor when I sang di Luna in *Il trovatore* with the same company. Now here we both were making our débuts with the New York Metropolitan Opera! Grace Bumbry is a wonderful singer, and even though I felt that *Tosca* was not a role that she was suited to, the performances were a tremendous success and especially for Levine who made an enormous impression with his dramatic grasp and out-standing technical control. In the cast we realised we had a real operatic conductor with immense flair and the most thorough knowledge of everything in the opera. During the rehearsals and the performances he mimed every word with me. He absolutely knew every word and note of the score from memory. I greatly respect a conductor who has those qualities.

The *Tosca* first performance was a matinée and so during the evening we were all at a party that was being given by Grace Bumbry's agent. During the party somebody suddenly came up to me and asked if he could speak with me. 'Mr Glossop,' he said 'my name is Sol Hurok. Can I ask you, are you represented in the United States?' I told him that my engagement at the Metropolitan Opera had been arranged by Sandor Gorlinsky. 'Oh yes,' he said, 'my dear friend Sandor, I understand. But please, if you might need any help at all in the United States, will you ring me first?' I could hardly believe it – Hurok was the most famous and powerful opera agent in the world. It was all a wonderful start to fifteen thrilling seasons singing at the Metropolitan Opera. I loved going there and I was treated extremely well. Apart from that aloof and cold response I had received from Rudolph Bing, I found the atmosphere at the Met highly congenial and friendly.

It was James Levine who asked if I would sing the title role in Berg's *Wozzeck* with him at the Metropolitan Opera in 1974. Although I was delighted with the idea of being offered such a demanding and challenging role, at first I was very apprehensive. I had never sung it before, although I had seen the opera when Geraint Evans had been Wozzeck at Covent Garden. It had struck me as being dramatically riveting but very tough and hard on the voice. I was not sure I would be able to handle it, and I wondered whether I really was cut out to perform the role of a poor, simple but psychotic soldier who is used and abused so vilely by almost everyone around him that he kills his wife and then commits suicide. But then I realised this was a very important opportunity to perform a great and fascinating masterpiece and take on a role that needs particularly powerful and searching acting from the singer. I decided I wanted to accept the offer, but there would have to be a deal. I would sing Wozzeck provided I could be given four performances of Scarpia during the rehearsal period! Cheeky maybe, but it worked. The Met said yes immediately.

Singing my first Wozzeck was indeed a huge challenge, but, as it turned out, it was one of the biggest successes of all for me at the Met. There are people who still tell me they felt it was one of the best performances I gave in the House. Of course, there was the added frisson and intensity of taking on a completely different kind of role, but at the same time, once I was able to take control of the very difficult vocal writing, I felt a huge thrill

Wozzeck, *New York Metropolitan Opera, 1972*

performing this immensely dramatic and disturbing opera. In one way, Wozzeck is similar to Rigoletto. He is a put-upon creature and you need to arouse the audience's deep sympathy for him, which I felt I could do. In fact I would go as far as to say that having sung *Rigoletto* so much, I had learned something vital for the performance of *Wozzeck*. That might raise some eyebrows, but the point is that in *Rigoletto* you have to go so much further than just conventional singing if you are going to convince the audience that the man is a tragic character. *Wozzeck* has nothing whatsoever in common with *Rigoletto* musically, but in terms of the approach to the performance there is a similar challenge. To convey his tragedy you have to go very much further than just sing the very angular and disturbing vocal lines.

I had to work very hard, though, to arrive at that point. Even today, more than three quarters of a century after its première, *Wozzeck* is hugely difficult to master and even listen to in some ways, and for a singer who had spent most of his career in the great romantic repertoire, vocally and musically it was like going right back to the beginning and starting again on something completely new. But I was very fortunate because there were superb music coaches and repetiteurs at the Metropolitan Opera, really not far behind the unique standard of the music staff at Covent Garden in Sir David Webster's time. Without them it would have been far harder and more dangerous. Even then, the psychological strain on the singer is particularly great when it comes to the performance of *Wozzeck*. There is virtually no let up in the tension and the blackness all the way through. Wozzeck is almost permanently disturbed, distressed and confused. He is a total and helpless victim – when he sees his wife dance with the Drum Major and laugh as he mauls her lecherously, he just has no idea what to do about it.

The production of *Wozzeck* by Herbert Graf, staged for the revival by Patrick Libby, was very powerful without in any way trying to alter or 'enhance' what had been originally stipulated by the composer, who was also the librettist. Most of the productions I took part in at the Metropolitan Opera were on the whole faithful to the original intentions of the composers and the librettists, and I have to say that I feel very strongly that in general this is the way opera should be performed. When an opera is set in a particular era, it takes into account and expresses how the people of that era were – what they believed in, what they feared, whether they were religious or not, and so on. Rigoletto is terrified when he is cursed by Monterone because people at that time, in the sixteenth century, were devastated by a curse. They even were at the time of the première of *Rigoletto*, in 1851. If a production of *Rigoletto* transfers the action out of that environment into a time where no one believes in the power of a curse, how can the libretto and music have any meaning? And what about operas that deliberately set out to create the atmosphere of a mythical existence? When Wagner wrote the *Ring Cycle* it was the middle of the nineteenth century, and people certainly did not believe then that a kingdom of gods ruled the world and valkyries rode through the air on horses. So if the *Ring* was accepted at its première as a fictitious, symbolic work, why can it not be acceptable as such today? There are instances when experimental productions and shifting the time of the action have been effective, but I think they have been rare.

*   *   *

The New York Metropolitan Opera became almost a second home for me for the remainder of my career. London was still my real home and in fact I had been able to buy a very luxurious house in Bishop's Avenue where Joyce and I lived in really prosperous conditions. We were both greatly in demand internationally and in truth we were both travelling far too much to be able to be together as much as we should have been – although we did sing together sometimes, and most memorably in Bari when Joyce was a glorious Amneris in *Aida*. It is very difficult to say 'no' when one is asked to perform roles one loves so much and there is also the excitement of being on stage in great theatres in great cities around the world. At the same time a singer must be careful and I learned this the hard way in 1972.

During a run of performances of *Billy Budd* at Covent Garden, I commuted to Barcelona to rehearse for a new production of Verdi's *Ernani*. This entailed being in Barcelona for *Ernani* on

12–14 January, London for *Budd* on the 15th and 17th, and Barcelona again for *Ernani* on the 18th, with the opening night on the 19th. The very next day my work continued in Barcelona with rehearsals for Verdi's *Luisa Miller*, which was to open on the 24th. In the meantime a further *Ernani* performance was scheduled during that week. I managed to survive up to the first night of *Ernani*, but then I began to realise I was in trouble. I had never sung the role of the Miller before and I had only three days of rehearsals, with the second *Ernani* performance in between them. There was just neither enough time nor space to prepare such a difficult and heavy part as the Miller. I really felt that this time I had expected too much of myself. On the opening night of *Luisa Miller* I was aware of my vocal tiredness and was very unhappy with my performance. Meanwhile I still had to sing *Ernani* once more and *Luisa Miller* twice before the end of my engagement, so I was forced to take them as carefully as I could. When I returned home to London on 4 February, I promised myself I would never again put my career at risk in such a manner. I realised very starkly how an artist must decide whether or not a tempting offer is practical and sensible to accept.

Later that year I returned to Salzburg to sing for the third consecutive season in a production of Verdi's *Otello* that was both conducted and directed by the supreme reigning king of music in Salzburg, Herbert von Karajan. In the cast was Jon Vickers as Otello, Mirella Freni as Desdemona and myself as Iago. This time the performances were followed by the making of an ambitious filmed production of the opera in the studios with Karajan supervising not only the music and staging but the filming as well, albeit with a number of assistant directors on hand. He was undoubtedly a very remarkable man and a great conductor, but I did not enjoy the experience of working

Iago from the film Otello *directed by*
Herbert von Karajan, with Jon Vickers as Otello

with him in *Otello*. There were some elements both in the staging and in the musical interpretation that I felt were contrary to Verdi's intentions and then when we came to make the film it was particularly difficult because he insisted we had to record the soundtrack first and mime the stage action to the recording afterwards. For the film, we had to spend an enormous amount of time just concentrating on synchronising everything perfectly, and to try to give a dramatic performance of an entire opera in these circumstances is extremely hard.

On the artistic side, the fact is that Karajan was a dictator. He was not a bully, in the way Solti was, but he was fundamentally authoritarian. Although he was a sympathetic accompanist, this was only within the context of his own artistic concept. There was no room for any difference of opinion. Actually we got on well on the whole, and he treated me very decently, but in the theatre in Salzburg I realised how dismissive he was of anyone else's viewpoint. There was an incident when Jon and I were right at the back of the stage whilst Mirella was practically on the edge at the front, and when I ventured to suggest to Karajan that this was making it very difficult to achieve a proper balance between the three of us, he just brushed the matter aside. Nevertheless I did respect him very much as he had such a great talent. In particular, the way he conducted the opening of the opera was riveting, and he was masterly in his handling of the music that begins the last act, preparing the scene of Desdemona's Willow Song.

Karajan was perhaps the first of the superstar conductors of the media, although some would say that Leopold Stokowski preceded him. Both conductors were deeply interested in the world of film and Stokowski was a great pioneer when he collaborated with Walt Disney in *Fantasia*. He also took part in other films and had a notorious affair with one of the great screen idols, Greta Garbo. I did not have an affair with any film celebrities, but during this particularly exciting time of my career I did have the opportunity of making the acquaintance of another screen 'goddess'.

In 1974, Patric Schmid, the founder and artistic director of Opera Rara, a specialist recording company publishing seldom performed operas, put on a gala concert in the Royal Albert Hall, and one of the people I was introduced to after the concert was the actor Charles Grey. He was a great friend of Ava Gardner, who was with him at the concert, which was taking place on her home territory, as she lived just opposite the Royal Albert Hall. She was giving a party that night and she invited my wife and me to come along. We had a fantastic evening and Joyce told me afterwards that at one moment Ava Gardner took her into her bedroom and said to her 'I don't suppose I could borrow Peter for this evening, could I?' 'Well that's entirely up to Peter,' she replied. Truly, that would not have been of any interest to me, despite what anyone might have thought or might think now! But it was special to meet Ava Gardner, who was a marvellous lady. She had personality, she was still beautiful, though no longer the star she once was, and she gave us a lovely after-concert soirée in wonderful style. It was a delightfully intimate little party as there cannot have been more than ten of us there.

Incidentally, Patric Schmid is still the director of the enter-prising Opera Rara, and by a happy coincidence our paths are meeting again after a long time, as I will explain later.

*   *   *

I sang a great deal of the music of my favourite Giuseppe Verdi throughout these two decades of world touring and in particu-lar I have fond memories of *I vespri Siciliani* in Paris, *Rigoletto* in Munich and *Macbeth* at a BBC Promenade Concert in London. Thereby hang some tales. A new production of *I vespri Siciliani* was being mounted in Paris in 1974 with Placido Domingo as Henri and myself as the French Governor of Sicily. I had never sung or even seen the opera and had to learn the big role of the Governor from scratch, so I was grateful there were several weeks of rehearsal, which I certainly needed. Unfortunately I developed a bad cold, as increasingly became the case as the years went by, and it worsened right up to the dress rehearsal, partly, I am sure, because of the so-called treatment I was receiving. The regular theatre doctor was away on holiday and the ancient man I saw instead just gave me some pills that were completely ineffectual. At the dress rehearsal I realised I could not sing the opening night and I asked Joan Ingpen in the opera management to get a replacement. Luckily the baritone who had sung the opera in Hamburg recently was free, but only

The French Governor of Sicily in I vespri Siciliani, *Paris 1974*

for the first three performances, so I was given leave to go back to London on condition I returned for the fourth performance.

Back in London I immediately had an appointment with Norman Punt, my ear, nose and throat specialist who unfailingly cured my problems. When he examined the medicine the French doctor had prescribed, he burst out laughing. 'Who is this doctor?' he asked, 'These are pills I give to elderly ladies with a touch of a cold. They would never cure your raging sore throat in a million years.' After ascertaining that I had never been given cortisone before, he treated me with it and within two days I was practically cured. I travelled back to Paris and felt ready for the performance. However . . .

There is a duet between Henri and the Governor in which a cut is often made, as the opera is very long and so is the duet. During the rehearsals, I had persuaded Placido and the conductor, Nello Santi, to perform the duet complete without a cut as it is such a fine one. On my opening night, which was now the fourth night in the opera house, we reached the point where the cut can be made and I suddenly found myself singing totally on my own with no orchestra. I was absolutely stunned. Then, suddenly Placido went in front of the conductor and they both started together. I immediately realised that in my absence the cut had been implemented after all, so I jumped to the place in the score where we now were and joined in with no trouble. What had happened was that the baritone who had replaced me had never sung the complete duet without the cut, and as there was no time for him to learn it, the cut was put back in again. Unfortunately nobody had remembered to tell me. They all apologised profusely in the interval, with everyone blaming everybody else, of course.

I have a great affection for Placido. He is a very genuine man. It was back in 1965 that my wife Joyce first sang with him in Fort Worth. She was then enjoying international fame as Carmen, and this was her American début in the role, with Placido singing Don José very early in his career. She found him a wonderful colleague, already very thoughtful and searching as an interpreter and warm and open as a man. Later Placido and I were to sing together many times and I have always remembered one particular occasion when we were both appearing at the Madrid Opera. We were performing Ponchielli's *La Gioconda* and one night as we came out of the theatre he said 'Peter, I want you to look up at that first-floor window across the road there – in that room I was born.' I had always thought he was Mexican, but then he told me that his

Joyce Blackham in the role of Carmen

parents were *zarzuela* artists and when Placido was a child the *zarzuela* operas were dying out in Spain but were very popular in Mexico. So the family moved there and that is where Placido grew up. Now that he was back in Spain he was renewing his Spanish citizenship. All this was about five years after he had started to rise to fame – before that he had been working enormously hard for many years learning his art and craft with the Mexico Opera and then with the Tel Aviv Opera.

Success never changed Placido. He always remained a wonderful, honest man and forever warm and generous. I have never told my wife this, but when Placido and I were appearing together in *La Bohème*, I had a new girl friend and I let him have my old girl friend, and the next time he went home he brought back two bottles of the finest Spanish red wine you can buy. As to his artistry, he is one of the world's finest performers and it is truly amazing how he has remained

With Roman Polanski, Munich 1976

in wonderful voice right up to the time I am writing this, in 2003.

The *Rigoletto* performances I sang in Munich two years later brought me together with the brilliant Roman Polanski. He was directing the production and it was quite an experience. He was at that time banned from the United States for allegedly sodomizing a young girl and was operating mainly in Europe. What a talented man! I admired him enormously and we got on tremendously well. He was really very imaginative and highly inventive, for my personal taste too much so, but he had an extraordinary understanding of the essence of the opera dramatically and musically, so I happily went along with his ideas most of the time. Here was a case where a degree of experimentation actually served the composer's opera in a special way. There were a few occasions where I felt I could not do what he asked, but when I told him he immediately accepted. Although he was demanding he never assumed a superior stance. He felt the artists were his colleagues. I found him very thoughtful and deep in his entire approach. We spent a lot of time together outside the performances and had dinner in each other's company many times during the three weeks of rehearsals and after the performances. He was most engaging and also a very serious person.

Two years later, in 1978, a highlight of London's Promenade Concert season was a then very rare performance of the original 1847 version of Verdi's *Macbeth*. This was one of a series of performances of Verdi operas that were being given in their original versions rather than their far more familiar revised versions, and they were all organised by the BBC and the Verdi scholar Julian Budden and conducted by John Matheson. There were a lot of rehearsals for this performance of *Macbeth* and in the cast we all needed them as this original version was new to us. At that time it was hardly ever given and it turned out that this performance was something of a trail-blazer, because the revival of interest in Verdi's early music was just about to begin – before long this 1847 version of *Macbeth* became more frequently performed. As I have said earlier, in the chapter on Verdi, there are a number of significant differences between the two versions and this really was a big challenge for all of us to present a Verdi opera that in a number of respects was unfamiliar to the audience and artists alike. I am particularly happy that, quite coincidentally with the publication of this book, the BBC's recording of the Prom performance of *Macbeth* on 25 July 1978 is being officially released for the first time, on the Opera Rara label.* On it you can hear Martina Arroyo's Lady Macbeth and the Macduff of

---

* The performance of Macbeth is issued by Opera Rara, catalogue number ORCV 301.

Kenneth Collins. It is the first part of a new series initiated by my old friend Patric Schmid – Opera Rara are releasing all those pioneering BBC performances of the Verdi operas in their original versions.

*   *   *

It felt like a homecoming after a very long time when I walked through the stage door of the London Coliseum in September 1980 to begin rehearsing in Strauss's *Arabella* with the English National Opera. The Sadlers Wells Company had moved to the Coliseum in 1968 and had become the English National Opera in 1974, and in truth it was now a very different company from the old Sadlers Wells where I grew up so happily in the 1950s. All the same it did feel to me like a return to the place where my career had burgeoned and there was now the added excitement of being able to take part in a new production during a particularly flourishing time in the company's history.

Lord Harewood and Sir Charles Mackerras had built up a brilliant new ensemble performing a very wide new repertoire to really high standards, and now the very gifted Music Director Mark Elder was also achieving superb results and spearheading some very ambitious if controversial productions. As was and mainly still is the Company's policy, the production of *Arabella* was to be sung in English. The opera was new to me and I was singing one of the heaviest roles I had ever undertaken, Mandryka, the wealthy but emotionally awkward landowner who finally finds true love with Arabella, the beautiful and understanding daughter of the impecunious Count Waldner. The work is so romantic and Mandryka is such a wonderful character that although I was at first concerned whether I should take it on, I soon felt I just could not refuse the offer.

I am so happy that I did accept the engagement as it turned out to be one of the happiest experiences of my career. I must admit that there were also a few sentimental reasons for this. My old friend Harold Blackburn was Arabella's father and we had a wonderful scene together; also the Arabella was Josephine Barstow, a great favourite of ENO audiences and she came from Sheffield! The producer was Dr Jonathan Miller, who came up with some very fine ideas, all of which I agreed to, and the conductor was Mark Elder. The performances were a really great success and I felt very moved each night, especially in the wonderful last scene when Arabella descends the stairs carrying a glass of water, which is the sign that she has accepted Mandryka's offer of marriage, finally transforming his whole life. It is one of Strauss's most beautiful moments.

After one of the performances, Lord Harewood asked if I would come and see him as he was interested to see if I was available to return to the ENO for another production. He was keen for me to sing some Wagner and I would have loved to do this because the company was in such splendid fettle. As it turned out there was a clash of dates and I just could not make myself available, but I took the opportunity of saying a few personal words to Lord Harewood, whom I greatly admired and liked. Whilst being so distinguished and authoritative he is one of the most approachable and liberal persons I have ever met and he has a wonderful sense of humour. 'I am ever so pleased to have had this opportunity of getting to know you,' I said, 'because you are just how I expect a Yorkshireman should be.' 'Actually I'm not a Yorkshireman,' he replied. 'But you are the Earl of Harewood,' I said. 'Yes that's true, but actually I was born in Buckingham Palace.' The way he said that was very amusing and it is typical of his humanity.

The performances of *Arabella* were to be my last appearances with the company that had nurtured my career and given me the finest possible introduction to professional opera singing. Although I was still very much enjoying a tremendously busy life singing in the world's top opera houses, life was changing in many ways and a few years down the road it would change dramatically. I was to pay an enormous price for the wonderful highs I had experienced and in fact already there had been a major change that in due course was to cost me particularly dearly. By now, I was divorced and had re-married and I was a father. I could not know that within five years I would be completely alone and would then have less than a year of my career left.

CHAPTER NINE

Goodbye to all That – Mostly

I had the most wonderful and unusual marriage to Joyce. We were both very individual people and followed our own tracks in a remarkably successful way. As two opera singers with our own very busy careers, we were not conventional husband and wife at all. We gave each other what I am sure was a rare degree of freedom and acceptance. For my part, Joyce was always an exceptionally understanding and supportive partner and for two decades I was blessed to have her as such a wife. Unfortunately, I made the mistake of falling in love with a young ballet dancer. It was in 1973 when I was at the height of my international success and still enjoying particularly happy times as a regular guest at the Royal Opera House Covent Garden. I was rehearsing *Don Giovanni* at Covent Garden, which in fact was to be my first Giovanni in London, as I had previously only sung the role in Dublin and Buenos Aires. An old friend of mine from the opera ballet in Sadlers Wells who was now with the Covent Garden opera ballet brought up this beautiful blonde with green eyes to introduce her to me, as she was to be my partner in the dancing which closes the first act.

Michelle Amos was only nineteen years old but I was very impressed when I met her and was only slightly miffed when my friend introduced me to her with the words 'This is your Don Giovanni, and I advise you not to believe a single word he

With Michelle, Amber and Rosie

says.' I soon became infatuated with Michelle and began to take her out. Joyce had no alternative but to divorce me. I know now that this was my disaster – but I did not know it at the time. In 1977 I married Michelle, who was twenty-six years younger than me, and for a time we were happy. We bought a lovely home in Teddington, where my new wife bore me two daughters, and whenever possible my family accompanied me around the world to my performances in the world's greatest cities.

It was not too long before I began to feel that I was not loved. I was right because in due course Michelle found a new man friend and there was no future at all for our marriage. We divorced in 1986 and ever since then I have been on my own –

and not only domestically. When the divorce actually came it was the climax of eighteen months in which it felt as though everything I had built up in my life was collapsing.

On New Year's Day 1985, I was in New York in the midst of what had been a particularly happy season at the Metropolitan Opera. Two and a half weeks earlier, on 15 December, I had sung the title role in *Simon Boccanegra* and at the end of the opera I had received a particularly warm reception. James Levine, who was conducting, put his arm round my shoulder and led me back to my dressing room in person. He then asked my dressers to leave and locked the door from the inside. We began to discuss the intricacies of performing the role of Boccanegra and I was touched that he was so complimentary about my performance. When he opened the door to leave, there was still a crowd of enthusiastic opera-goers waiting to see me. I was a very happy baritone.

There were then a few more performances of the opera that I was assigned to cover, after which came my next performance on stage as Boccanegra, on 1 January. Feeling confident after the success of my first performance, at the beginning of the opera I really let myself go in the Prologue and then even more so in the recognition scene with Amelia, Boccanegra's daughter. Then came the scene after that, the Council Chamber, which is the heaviest in the entire opera for Boccanegra – he dominates the whole action in it. To my dismay, when I reached my first high G, my voice cracked. I immediately realised my voice was tired, but I still had a long way to go. Although I did what I could to protect the vocal chords, it was obvious to me that I was in deep trouble. When I came to my big solo 'Plebe, Patrizi, Popolo', where the Doge (Boccanegra) passionately implores all the warring parties to come together in love and peace, I was singing with only half my voice. I finished the

With Amber   *Amber and Rosie*

scene as well as I could manage and was then glad to have thirty minutes rest before my next appearance, which is the scene where the Doge drinks poison that Paolo has prepared for him. I was particularly grateful to be poisoned on this occasion because I had an excuse for my failing voice! I managed to finish the opera but I recognized that my career with the New York Metropolitan Opera was coming to a close. We have a saying in our profession: 'you are only as good as your last performance'.

In the most recent previous seasons at the Met I had been covering more roles as an understudy than actually singing performances on stage. I really should have been more diligent with myself and requested more stage singing, and I should also have been asking myself more closely why I was not being offered as many parts as before for the performances. After so many continuing years of successes one can easily forget that one has grown a lot older and the world has also moved on. I had appeared every season at the Met for fifteen years, and I had become too confident that life would just continue as it had been. As I had been doing so much covering in the most recent years, my voice had not been used enough, and just a few rehearsals a week were not enough to keep the vocal muscles strong. The ideal schedule is to sing two performances a week to keep in shape. I have always maintained that an opera singer is like a sportsman, except that the sportsman must keep his whole body in shape whereas the singer only needs to concentrate on his vocal muscles in such an active way. And like a sportsman, once a sign of serious weakness is seen, it is often very difficult to recover the confidence of the public and the promoters. After that second performance of *Simon Boccanegra* I worked very hard on my voice, and I never lost it again in a performance, but the damage was done.

For the remainder of 1985 and the following year, there was less and less singing on the stage of the Metropolitan Opera and indeed elsewhere. Actually there had already been quite a fall back internationally for a few years. I had not sung at Covent Garden for five years and I had not been back to Europe since 1983. It was now the twilight of my career, and yet despite my awareness both of this and also of my deteriorating second marriage, I was still then not prepared for the inevitable finale that within a year was to bring about the biggest change of my life.

On 8 December 1985 I finished a run of performances of the role of Mr Redburn in *Billy Budd* at the San Francisco Opera. When I arrived back two days later Michelle immediately told me she wanted a divorce. During the next several months my life consisted mainly of commuting to New York to cover and still sometimes sing performances and trying to live in a home where my wife's one source of conversation was the coming divorce and the share of proceeds from our house which would have to be sold. In August 1986 I went to Los Angeles to sing Sharpless in Puccini's *Madam Butterfly* for the new Los Angeles Opera Company and when I returned I finally realised that my life was going to change dramatically – and soon. I accepted that the divorce was inevitable and I recognised that my career was no longer what it had been. I spent a lot of time with my friend Craig Sullivan, who was the manager of a lovely country-style pub in Axminster, Devon, and I began to search for a retirement cottage in the district. I was fortunate to find exactly what I was looking for in Hawkchurch, a village just outside Axminster.

I returned to Los Angeles for a few more performances of *Madam Butterfly*, on 8, 11 and 14 October 1986, and by now I had decided these would be the last appearances of my career. On my return to England I announced my retirement from the theatre and the world of opera. It was a hard and painful decision to make, but with the divorce and the loss of my home there was no alternative.

On 25 November 1986 I left my home in Teddington for the last time, leaving my two daughters in the safe keeping of their mother, and came down to my beautiful new home in Devon. I am alone and often sad but I have never regretted the move. For all I have lost, after seventeen years I still enjoy every day I walk into my house. And there is a special and perhaps, for the reader, a surprising finale. I will always regret the folly which led to my first divorce, but I have been extraordinarily fortunate. Joyce and I never lost touch after we divorced and in fact we never fell out as friends. She was always able to draw men who wanted to marry her and indeed she married again twice, finding remarkable husbands and then paying dearly when the marriages ended tragically. Through all these immense highs and lows, and mine too, our friendship never died and now, in my last and often lonely years, Joyce is loyal and caring to me in a way that I think few former husbands in this world will have experienced from a former wife. Joyce now has a wonderful partner and they live not too far away from my home, which is a lifeline for me, as I am out of touch with nearly all the world in which I was once so immensely involved and of which I was so privileged and honoured to be a part.

Some days that fantastic, unique world seems so far away and long ago, and at other times it lives incredibly thrillingly and vividly for me as though it were yesterday. As I write this, it is close on seventeen years since I last stood on the operatic stage. Maybe I might have gone on singing longer than I did, and Joyce certainly felt I should have done, even though we knew I would no longer be able to have the kind of career I had enjoyed before. But with the break-up of my second marriage I lost my faith. I just did not feel I could go on singing and so I decided the time had come to leave the life I had so passionately loved for nearly forty years.

*   *   *

In the last quarter of the twentieth century opera changed vastly in many ways, and even since my retirement much has changed. Very few singers now come up the way I did, beginning in the chorus of a company, then spending many long years learning a large repertoire as part of an ensemble. For one thing there are far fewer ensemble companies now. Jet travel is one reason for this. Since the early 1970s, successful young singers have wanted to fly all over the world and take international engagements – naturally. And then there is less and less money available to run companies with really good regular ensembles and teams of expert music staff. There are exceptions, like Valery Gergiev's Kirov Opera, but even in that company there are difficulties and restrictions the like of which would have made life much harder than it was for Norman Tucker and Sir David Webster in the balmy old days of Sadlers Wells and Covent Garden.

I think the most significant changes of all, though, have been the attitudes to productions – and increasingly so in the last two decades. During this time it has become expected that the majority of new productions should take a completely new look at the story, the characters and action, quite often to the point of departing radically from the composers' and librettists' original intentions. This poses a completely new kind of situation for young and for that matter established singers of today in comparison to how it was in opera as recently as thirty years ago. They are now faced with having to reassess their work on a far greater scale than I ever had to in my day. Stage directors have more and more power and with it they more and more wish to impose massive changes to the original. The latter part of my career overlapped with the rush of new-style productions, and I have already said in this book how, on the whole, I could not and cannot accept them because I believe that most of them are seriously at odds with the true feelings and meanings of the music and libretti. However, this is how it is now and I know there are some young singers who are in favour.

There are some wonderfully talented singers today, of course – more and more of them reach such a high standard so quickly. But it does worry me that their rise to fame is so often determined by competitions, when we cannot really tell if they are true stage animals. In fact if I have one general criticism today it is that in my experience not enough young singers have learned that opera is not just about beautiful singing. The sound in the voice in a particular passage must come from the meaning and feeling of the words. For this reason it cannot always be beautiful. I feel there is too much concentration now on just vocal technique. A lovely and beautiful phrase is just not enough. I was very impressed when I saw on television the young baritone who was the winner of the BBC Cardiff Singer of the World competition this year, 2003, but I felt my old criticism coming out again: he had a wonderful voice and fine artistry but not enough variety of expression. There was plenty of vocal power, but when he sang Ford's monologue from Verdi's *Falstaff*, if he would have allowed himself to put some tenor colour into his splendid baritone he would have projected more expression.

But thank goodness opera still lives and that young people still want to become opera singers! When I see them, admittedly nearly always only on television and video these days, I thank the great composers who have made it all happen. They gave opera singers the privilege of performing their works of genius. I always felt so privileged to have been given the opportunities I had in my career and I honestly think that I made the most of them. I loved my life in opera so greatly. For me there is no finer feeling in the whole world than being on the stage of an international opera house, backed by a fine orchestra and great fellow artists, and having the honour of interpreting great operatic roles such as Rigoletto, Rodrigo, Iago, Simon Boccanegra or Falstaff. Those roles are all in operas written by the great master Giuseppe Verdi. I have sung the works of a huge range of composers and enormously enjoyed the finest ones, but for me Verdi's operas are the most special. Here I speak as a baritone, because Verdi gave a new emphasis to the baritone voice. He wrote for a higher *tessitura* than had previous composers, giving it a new passion and drama in opera. His baritone roles were more complicated than ever before, with a greater range of character shades. This gave him the opportunity to express a greater span of emotions in them, and it gave the baritone performer a new scope of variation and creativity on stage. To Verdi I owe one of my greatest debts. But of course there are other debts – to my mother, without whom I certainly would never have become an opera singer, to my first wife Joyce for the care and love she gave me, to Norman Tucker and David Webster at Sadlers Wells and Covent Garden respectively, and indeed to more people to whom I apologise for not mentioning them in person here. They all contributed so crucially to the wonderful life I had as an opera singer.

I began writing this book to let my two daughters, Amber and Rosie, know who their father was as they were not even born when I was at the height of my career. I hope I have been able to convey to them and other readers what a fantastic world I had the honour and privilege of being a part of. The story of this Yorkshire baritone is now over. Thank you for sharing it with me.

Index of Musical Works

A Midsummer Night's Dream (Britten), 64, 66, 73, 131

Andrea Chenier (Giordano), 59

Arabella (R. Strauss), 13, 14, 155, 156

Billy Budd (Britten), 15, 100, 131, 133–138, 145, 162

Carmen (Bizet), 30, 41, 46, 151

Die Fledermaus (J. Strauss), 39, 47

Don Carlos (Verdi), 27, 66, 73, 83–86, 98, 115

Don Giovanni (Mozart), 42, 50, 65, 158

Erlkönig (Schubert), 24

Ernani (Verdi), 31, 145, 146

Eugene Onegin (Tchaikovsky), 13, 55–58, 114, 115, 132

Falstaff (Verdi), 87, 120, 166

I Pagliacci (Leoncavallo), 26, 32, 40, 48, 49, 63, 73, 93, 115, 116

I vespri Siciliani (Verdi), 149

Il trovatore (Verdi), 32, 50, 51, 54, 63, 73, 86, 88, 98, 100–102, 110, 141

Katya Kabanova (Janáček), 40

La Bohème (Puccini), 41, 48, 72, 73, 75, 77, 79, 80, 83, 85, 110, 152

La traviata (Verdi), 38, 41, 44, 47, 55, 71–73, 89, 108, 130

Lohengrin (Wagner), 73–75

Luisa Miller (Verdi), 117, 146

Macbeth (Verdi), 15, 24, 119–121, 149, 154

Madame Butterfly (Puccini), 41, 163

Merrie England (German), 59

Mignon (Thomas), 31

Otello (Verdi), 27, 73, 98, 100, 108, 109, 116, 120, 124–126, 128, 129, 140, 146, 147

Rigoletto (Verdi), 25, 26, 32, 47, 55, 58, 59, 64, 65, 68, 72–74, 90–93, 95–98, 100, 101, 103, 104, 106–112, 114, 117, 121–123, 137, 140, 143–145, 149, 153, 166

Roberto Devereux (Donizetti), 92, 115

Samson and Delilah (Saint-Saëns), 37, 38

Simon Boccanegra (Verdi), 15, 114, 130, 160, 162, 166

Tannhäuser (Wagner), 61, 81, 82

The Pearl Fishers (Bizet), 44, 46

The Ring Cycle (Wagner), 46, 81, 100, 145

The Tales of Hoffman (Offenbach), 29

Tosca (Puccini), 59, 60, 72, 73, 86, 90, 140, 141

Turandot (Puccini), 73, 74

Un ballo in maschera (Verdi), 42, 43, 68, 70, 71, 104–106, 115

Wozzeck (Berg), 142–144

Biographical index

Amos, Michelle, 1954– Second wife of Peter Glossop, 158, 159, 162

Arundel, Dennis, 1898–1988 English actor, composer, producer and writer for theatre, radio, television and film, 59, 60

Baker, Dame Janet, 1933– English contralto, 62

Barstow, Dame Josephine, 1940– English soprano, 156

Bastianini, Ettore, 1922–1967 Italian baritone, 68–70, 111

Baylis, Lilian, 1874–1937 English theatre manager, founder of Vic-Wells (later Sadlers Wells) Opera and Ballet companies, 35

Besch, Anthony, 1924–2002 English stage director, 59

Bing, Sir Rudolph, 1902–1997 Austrian/English impresario and intendant, General Manager of the New York Metropolitan Opera 1950–1972, 140, 142

Blackburn, Harold, 1925–1981 English bass baritone, 51, 156

Blackham, Joyce, 1934– English mezzo-soprano, first wife of Peter Glossop, 25, 30, 43, 44, 47, 48, 51–54, 58, 92, 96, 110, 133, 141, 145, 148, 151, 152, 158, 159, 162–164, 167

Bogianchino, Massimo, 1922– Italian administrator, pianist and musicologist, Intendant of the Rome Opera House 1968–1972 and Intendant of the La Scala Milan Opera 1972–1979, 114, 115

Britten, Benjamin, 1913–1976   English composer, conductor and pianist, founder of the English Opera Group and the Aldeburgh Festival, 15, 36, 64, 66, 74, 100, 131-133, 135, 136, 138

Bumbry, Grace, 1937–   American mezzo-soprano, 140, 141

Callas, Maria, 1923–1977   American/Greek soprano, 36, 67, 77, 90

Carreras, Jose, 1946–   Spanish tenor, 79

Christoff, Boris, 1914–1993   Bulgarian bass, 36, 67

Coleman, Basil, 1916–   English theatre and television stage director, 135

Cossutta, Carlo, 1932–   Italian tenor, 90

Craig, Charles, 1919–1997   English tenor, 18, 59, 72, 87, 163

D'Averio, Gabriele   Italian opera agent, 87, 88, 98, 108, 110, 111, 115

Davis, Sir Colin, 1927–   English conductor, Music Director of Sadlers Wells Opera 1959–1963, Music Director of Royal Opera House Covent Garden 1971–1986, Principal Conductor London Symphony Orchestra 1995– , 59

Devine, George, 1910–1966   English actor and producer, 55

Di Stefano, Giuseppe, 1921–   Italian tenor, 85

Domingo, Placido, 1941–   Spanish tenor and conductor, 149

Downes, Sir Edward, 1924–   English conductor, scholar and translator, Music Director of the Australian Opera 1972–1976, 16, 69, 81, 84, 95–97

Elder, Mark, 1947–   English conductor, Music Director of English National Opera 1979–1993, 155, 156

Evans, Sir Geraint, 1922–1992   Welsh baritone, 34, 90, 142

Biographical index

Fischer-Dieskau, Dietrich, 1925–   German baritone, conductor and writer, 125

Freni, Mirella, 1935–   Italian soprano, 100, 146

Gardner, Ava, 1922–1990   American film actress, 148, 149

Gardner, John, 1917–   English composer, conductor and professor, 36

Gergiev, Valery, 1953–   Russian conductor, Chief Conductor and Artistic Director of the Kirov Opera 1988–, 164

Ghiaurov, Nicolai, 1929–   Bulgarian bass, 84, 85

Glossop, Amber, 1979–   Daughter of Peter Glossop, 159, 160, 163, 167

Glossop, Cyril, 1900–1933   Father of Peter Glossop, 21–26, 54

Glossop, Doreen, 1930–   Sister of Peter Glossop, 21, 24, 25, 34, 35, 40, 53, 54

Glossop, Harry, 1925–1941   Brother of Peter Glossop, 21, 25, 54

Glossop, Rosie, 1981–   Daughter of Peter Glossop, 159, 160, 163, 167

Glossop, Violet Elizabeth, 1906–1957   Mother of Peter Glossop, 21-26, 28, 52–54, 167

Gobbi, Tito, 1913–1984   Italian baritone, 67, 89, 90, 96, 97, 103, 107, 128, 140

Goodall, Sir Reginald, 1901–1990   English conductor, 81–83

Gorlinsky, Sandor   Polish/English impressario, 85, 87, 108, 115, 141

Graf, Herbert, 1904–1973   Austrian/American stage director and administrator, 144

Grey, Charles, 1928–2000   English stage and film actor, 148

Harewood, Earl of, 1923– English administrator, intendant, writer and critic, Artistic Director of the Edinburgh Festival 1961–1965, Managing Director of English National Opera 1972–1982, 13, 14, 132, 155, 156

Hislop, Joseph, 1884–1977 Scottish tenor, 48, 50

Hurok, Sol, 1888–1974 Russian/American impressario, 141

Jones, Dame Gwyneth, 1937– Welsh soprano, 101, 110

Karajan, Herbert von, 1908–1989 Austrian conductor and stage director, Principal Conductor and Artistic Director of the Berlin Philharmonic Orchestra 1955–1989, Artistic Director of the Vienna State Opera 1956–1964, Artistic Director of the Salzburg Festival 1964–1989, 100, 115, 116, 146–148

Klemperer, Otto, 1885–1973 German conductor, composer and stage director, Artistic Director of the Berlin Kroll Opera 1927–1931, Principal Conductor of the Philharmonia (later New Philharmonia) Orchestra 1959–1972, 67, 74, 75

Levine, James, 1943– American conductor, Music Director of the New York Metropolitan Opera 1975– , 141, 142, 160

Lockhart, James, 1930– Scottish conductor, Music Director of Welsh National Opera 1968–1973, 65

Mackerras, Sir Charles, 1925– Australian conductor and scholar, Music Director of the Sadlers Wells, later English National, Opera 1970–1977, 15, 16, 39, 135, 155

Magiera, Leone Italian pianist and singing teacher, 86

Matheson, John, 1928– New Zealand conductor, 69, 81, 116, 154

McNeil, Cornel, 1922– American baritone, 105, 106

Menotti, Gian Carlo, 1911– Italian/American composer and stage director, 108, 109

Miller, Sir Jonathan, 1934–   English stage director and writer, 117, 146, 156

Moffo, Anna, 1932–   American soprano, 90, 92–95

Moore, Appleton   English singing teacher, 38, 49, 50

Mosley, Leonard   English singing teacher, 27, 28

Mudie, Michael, 1914–1962   English conductor, 39

Pavarotti, Luciano, 1935–   Italian tenor, 77–79, 86, 87, 108, 112

Pears, Sir Peter, 1910–1986   English tenor, 74, 132, 135, 138

Polanski, Roman, 1933–   French/Polish film director, scriptwriter, actor, 153

Rich, Eva   English theatre company director, 29, 30

Robertson, James, 1912–1991   English conductor, 39, 82

Santi, Nello, 1931–   Italian conductor, 151

Schippers, Thomas, 1930–1977   American conductor, 109

Sharp, Frederick, 1911–1988   English baritone, 49

Siciliani, Francesco, 1911–   Italian music administrator and composer, Intendant of the La Scala Milan Opera 1957–1972 and 1980–1983, 108, 110, 111, 115, 149

Sillem, Maurits, 1929–2002   English conductor, 80, 81

Solti, Sir Georg, 1912–1997   Hungarian conductor, Music Director of the Royal Opera House Covent Garden 1961–1971, Music Director of the Chicago Symphony Orchestra 1971–1993, 77, 83, 90–95, 147

Sutherland, Dame Joan, 1926–   Australian soprano, 67

Tucker, Norman, 1910–1978   Director of Opera at Sadlers Wells 1947–1951, Director of Sadlers Wells Theatre 1951–1966, 32, 35, 36, 40, 51, 59, 60, 65, 68, 71, 73, 76, 165, 167

Vaughan, Elisabeth, 1936–   Welsh soprano, 62, 78, 95

Vickers, Jon, 1926–   Canadian tenor, 67, 70, 82, 97, 98, 100, 140, 146

Visconti, Luchino, 1906–1978   Italian stage and film director, 67, 83, 98, 101

Vishnevskaya, Galina, 1926–   Russian soprano, 74, 75, 78, 97, 132

Ward, David, 1922–1983   Scottish bass, 40, 44, 74, 84

Webster, Sir David, 1903–1971   English intendant, founder and General Administrator of the Royal Opera House Covent Garden 1946–1970, 35, 36, 64, 66–68, 73, 76, 77, 83, 85, 86, 97, 101, 110, 144, 165, 167

Zeffirelli, Franco, 1923–   Italian opera, film and theatre producer and designer, 89–91, 93, 101

Printed in the United Kingdom
by Lightning Source UK Ltd.
100917UKS00001B/179-216